COLLECTED POEMS

NORMAN NICHOLSON
Collected Poems

EDITED WITH AN INTRODUCTION
BY NEIL CURRY

faber and faber

This edition first published in 2008
by Faber and Faber Ltd
3 Queen Square, London WC1N 3AU

Printed by CPI Antony Rowe, Eastbourne

A CIP record for this book is available from the British Library

ISBN 978-0-571-24328-0

Contents

NO STAR ON THE WAY BACK:
Ballads and Carols (1967)

A LOCAL HABITATION (1972)

Note

The texts of the poems are printed here in the forms in which they first appeared in the separate collections. The changes which Nicholson made for the *Selected Poems* of 1966 and 1982 are indicated in Textual Variations (pp. 439?40).

Acknowledgements

I would like to thank Philip Gardner, Stella Halkyard, and Bessie Schiff for their kindness and for the help which they have given me. A very special thank you must also go to Andrew F. Wilson who is working on a Bibliography of Norman Nicholson and whose assistance to me on many occasions has been selfless and invaluable.

Introduction

When Norman Nicholson died in 1987, an obituary in *The Times* described him as 'the most gifted English Christian provincial poet of his century', which is a true and a fair description, and yet, as all those adjectives come cluttering along together, how limiting, and how smugly patronizing they can begin to seem. They were words which Nicholson had grown grimly used to, and which he had himself sometimes flaunted because he understood their power, but he was also fully aware of the minefields of prejudice that lay behind them.

Even today it may not be uncommon for the rich and the titled to live out their days in the same great house, but a great house is one thing; a few cramped little rooms behind a shop-front in a narrow terraced street, even if those rooms are book-lined and snug, are another matter altogether. Yet that is how Nicholson lived. His father had been a gentleman's outfitter, with a shop at 14 St George's Terrace in Millom, a small, working-class town on the coast of what was then called Cumberland. Norman Nicholson was born there on 8 January 1914, and this was to be his home for every one of his seventy-three years. He was therefore, by definition, a provincial. But definitions necessarily seek to remain neutral; usage is where the battles are fought, and in 1954, in a broadcast entitled *On Being a Provincial*, Nicholson took up the challenge:

> If you want to annoy a man who comes from the provinces, call him a provincial. For the word, used in this sense, implies the smug, the narrow, the short-sighted; implies a mere second-hand, second-rate, out-of-date existence, a bad copy of the life of the capital.

This was his opening. He then went on the offensive, providing his own definition of a provincial as someone who lives in the place where his parents live, where his friends and relatives live, where there is a shared culture; and arguing that this is exactly what the metropolis lacks: 'Instead of a community we find an enormous heterogeneous collection of people gathered from all corners of the country and deposited like silt at the delta of a great river.' An artist in the metropolis, he said, will always feel isolated and set apart from the rest of mankind, and no wonder when the vast majority of mankind does not belong to a metropolis, but is provincial and always has been, finding its true identity in small, separate, ingrown communities. And after suggesting that 'it is precisely here, in our intense concern with what is close to us, that we most resemble the people of other countries and other times', he concluded with the assertion that the provincial 'may be all the more aware of that which is enduring in life and society'. Already we can begin to see where Nicholson's particular strength lies.

Of course it has to be said that he was blessed with a very exceptional provincial birthplace, and he knew it. 'I thank God for a lifetime spent in that same town' are the words with which he brings to an end his autobiography *Wednesday Early* Closing. Millom had provided him with so much of the material for his poetry and for his prose works too. In its geography, its history and its natural history, the area could hardly be richer. Millom itself is dominated by the 'bald, blank forehead' of Black Combe, an outcrop of Skiddaw slate, the oldest of the Lakeland rocks, and from his own window Nicholson had as a skyline Scafell Pike, Crinkle Crags and Coniston Old Man. Not far away are the megalithic stone circle at Swinside and the remains of the Roman port of Ravenglass. Further up the coast are the sandstone cliffs of St Bees, alive with kittiwakes and guillemots each spring, and then, in total contrast, come the towers of Sellafield. And Millom has its own history too. In 1860, less than two miles south of the town, the richest ever vein of haematite iron ore was discovered. An 'iron rush' followed. The town grew, output grew, and the slagbank grew, until suddenly in 1968 the government closed down the ironworks, and Millom (not that the rest of the country cared) knew unemployment and recession long before anywhere else. A great industry had boomed and burst in living memory. These are the sources that Norman Nicholson drew on.

If the area has any drawback, it could be said to be almost too rich in literary associations. But Nicholson assiduously avoided that. His first collection, *Five Rivers*, does concern itself with the landscape, but it is not the landscape of the Lake District Tourist Board. The place names are not the familiar ones. Instead of Hawkshead and Windermere, we have Egremont, Whitehaven, Eskmeals and Askam. This is the Cumbria where the Industrial Revolution began, and the landscape in *Egremont* is one where

> The damp autumnal sunlight drips
> On chimneys, pit-shafts, rubble-tips.

One could regard a predilection for such things as being part of the fashion of the times. In a conversation with David Wright (*PN Review* No. 46,1985), Nicholson acknowledged his early debt to Auden, and the way Auden had 'turned to the industrial scene', and he (mis) quoted those famous lines in *Letters To Iceland*:

> Clearer than Scafell Pike, my mind [sic] has stamped on
> The view from Birmingham to Wolverhampton.

The difference between the two poets, I would suggest, is that Auden, very much a man-on-the-move in those days, sees that view from a railway train window, and his attitude towards it is, as Nicholson recognizes, 'clearly romantic', while Nicholson himself has his feet on the ground. He lives there. He knows the place at first hand. He knows the local history. He knows about Will Ritson, the landlord of what is now the Wasdale Head Inn, who claimed to be the biggest liar in England, but at the same time he knows the more unromantic truths, such as the way the war effort in 1944 had pumped new economic life into places like Cleator Moor. The War is very much present in that first collection.

There is another element in *Five Rivers* which may come as something of a surprise to readers who only know Nicholson through his *Selected Poems*, and that is the very positive Christian commitment expressed there. The strength of this commitment may be seen even more plainly in a previously unpublished poem 'Now that I have made my decision' (p. 406) which was written in 1940; and in 1942, two years before the appearance of his own first collection, he was invited by Penguin Books to edit *An Anthology of Religious Verse Designed for the Times*, a truly perceptive anthology which brings together poets as seemingly disparate as Eliot and Auden, David Gascoyne, Charles Williams, Dylan Thomas, Andrew Young and Tambimuttu.

Nicholson's upbringing had not been *strictly* religious in the extreme sense, but his stepmother was an active Methodist who played the organ in Millom's Wesleyan Chapel, and as he explains in *Wednesday Early Closing* the Chapel was not simply where the family went to worship, it was the centre of their social lives: their club, their music-hall. It was also where the young Norman gained his early local fame as a reciter of poetry, a local fame, as he ruefully admitted, far greater than any he was later to acquire as a poet.

The move from the Chapel to the Church of England took place when he was about fifteen, and seems to have had an element of pragmatism about it, for it was then commonly believed that – as Nicholson put it – 'you had a much better chance of entering college if you had been confirmed.' But his true faith was firm and lasting. In 1966 he concluded his contribution to a collection of essays entitled *They Became Christians* with the words: 'If I am asked why I became a Christian, the only true answer is that I don't see how I could have helped it.'

One interesting aspect of the religious poems in *Five Rivers* is the way they foreshadow the approach Nicholson was to adopt in his plays of the 1950s, in that Bible stories are given a distinctly Cumbrian setting, so that when, for example, Elijah is fed by the ravens he is found to be out on the fells among 'the lyle herdwicks' and rowan trees and hawthorn.

Nicholson's second collection *Rock Face* is oddly disappointing. It does not follow up on the strengths of the earlier poems and could even be mistaken for the work of a much younger poet. It is as though there has been a failure of nerve. The one poem about Millom could be about almost anywhere. It is a distinctly literary volume, with poems about Caedmon, Cowper, Gray and Emily Brontë. It carries echoes of other poets and veers uncomfortably in manner between the austerity of Eliot and the high-flown tones of Dylan Thomas. The syntax wriggles self-consciously and the imagery lacks that precision which had once invited us to see a globe-flower as being 'like a lemon, quartered but unpeeled'. It is ominous too that a quarter of these poems have the word *Song* in their title; whatever else Nicholson was, he was never a singer. It is hardly surprising that only two items from *Rock Face* were included in the 1982 *Selected Poems*.

But six years later came *The Pot Geranium*, the title poem of which is one of the finest Nicholson ever wrote and a confident assertion that he had found his way again. He has drawn back into his own resources and into his own place. Not only is he back in Millom, he is on his own bed in the attic room of St George's Terrace. Outside he can see a red boxkite straining on its string high over the rooftops, but he turns away from it to consider the red geranium in its tiny pot on the windowsill. It is alive and he is alive. What more does he need? There are no limitations here:

And what need therefore
To stretch for the straining kite? – for kite and flower
Bloom in my room for ever; the light that lifts them
Shines in my own eyes, and my body's warmth
Hatches their red in my veins. It is the Gulf Stream
That rains down the chimney, making the soot spit; it is the
    Trade Wind
That blows in the draught under the bedroom door.
My ways are circumscribed, confined as a limpet
To one small radius of rock; yet
I eat the equator, breathe the sky, and carry
The great white sun in the dirt of my finger-nails.

Nicholson is now able to accept his own 'one small radius of rock' as a microcosm of the whole world and is able to convince us of it too. It is significant that those challenging words from *On Being A Provincial* were broadcast in the same year that *The Pot Geranium* was published, and the book itself gives us a detailed geography of this 'rock': King Street, Queen Street, Market Street and Station Yard, the Spiritualist Room, the garage and the licensed grocer's. The poet is now so much at home that his Bible stories are enacted not only in Cumbria, but in Millom itself, on the allotments ('A Turn for the Better').

In the poem 'On My Thirty-fifth Birthday' Nicholson seems to be remembering all those 'songs' in *Rock Face* and to be rejecting them.

There is no time now for words,
Unless the words have meaning; no time for poetry,
Unless the poem has a purpose; no time for songs,
But songs of work and wild methodical hymns.

The Pot Geranium is a collection in which purpose and meaning are unmistakable and it ends with what is arguably its author's most ambitious poem 'The Seven Rocks'. Here the themes of faith and place combine in a series of meditations in which the rocks forming the geological structure of the Lake District are presented as an analogy for the seven traditional Christian virtues; the virtues themselves coming to indicate in their turn qualities which Nicholson finds in the rocks.

Curiously, for the all the assurance of *The Pot Geranium*, there followed another crisis of confidence, and Nicholson did not produce another collection for eighteen years. It seemed to him that he had said all that there was to be said about Millom and that he could not go on repeating himself. He turned to prose, and these were the years which saw the publication of *The Lakers, Provincial Pleasures, Portrait of The Lakes, and Greater Lakeland*. But then, in 1959, he came upon what might seem, for Nicholson, a most unlikely inspiration – Robert Lowell's *Life Studies*. As he later told David Wright, 'I suddenly realized that there was a whole new area that I hadn't touched. I'd written about the rocks and the mines, but I hadn't written about my family. And that was the book which switched me from the town to the inhabitants as it were. And really started the last phase of my poetry, which I suppose all old men think is the best.'

And it was not only his family that he began to write about; he began to write about himself. 'The Whisperer', for instance, refers to what was perhaps the most important single event in his life: when at the age of sixteen he was found to have tuberculosis of the larynx and was sent away to a sanatorium in Hampshire, where he spent fifteen months in bed and was forbidden to speak. He lay there and read and thought and read and thought. It was his university, he said, and he often speculated that if he had really gone to university he would probably have come out and been a teacher and not written any poetry at all.

The title *A Local Habitation* is brilliantly defiant. The battle over 'the provincial' has been won. There had been people in *The*

Pot Geranium, but now they had come to the fore – the poet's grandmother, his father, his uncles and friends – and we hear them speak in their own words:

> 'There's nowt to be scared about,' she said,
> 'A big lad like you.'
> > ('Boo to a Goose')

> 'It's mending worse,' he said.
> > ('Old Man at a Cricket Match')

and

> 'I gave him an?*err*,' my father said.
> > ('Great Day')

It is this that gives the collection its distinctive tone. The manner is not a bit like Lowell and we might never have guessed the connection. These poems are colloquial, light-hearted, witty and warmly human, and *provincial*, about 'a small, self-contained and rather isolated community where you can hardly throw a penny into a crowd without hitting someone you are related to.'

The most striking thing about the final collection *Sea To The West* is that it is *not* an old man's book. There is some looking back (naturally enough) and an elegiac tone is occasionally struck (and why not?) but in so many other respects this is innovatory work. For one thing it looks different: the lines are often so much shorter – with the introduction of a punchy two-stress line that Nicholson claimed he had learned from Walter de la Mare. Also the poet's own speaking voice is much more in evidence, possibly because the sometime boy-reciter, famous in the old days in Millom, was popular once more on the reading circuits of the 1960s, and enjoying it immensely.

The only unquestionably 'Millom' poem in this collection is 'On The Dismantling of Millom Ironworks' and it stems from Wordsworth's observation that the area was, as he saw it, 'remote from every taint of sordid industry'. The irony, as Nicholson saw it, was that the whole process had turned full circle. The ironworks had been closed down and cleared away, and there was Black Combe again, and the shelducks could fly to their old feeding grounds without great chimneys in the way any more. But rather than prompting Ozymandias-like reflections or wistfulness about the transience of things, this led Nicholson to consider the permanence of the natural world – the way Halley's Comet has kept coming back for other eyes to see it, and the likelihood that when there are no eyes left to see, there will still be Black Combe and Scafell Pike.

In one of his reminiscences, 'At The Music Festival', Nicholson recalls how a local baritone, regardless of tone or tune, won the hearts of the local audience by the way he

> Hurled his voice like an iron quoit
> Clean into the Adjudicator's
> Union-Jacked box at the back.

He was, as they used to say, 'giving it Wigan'. In *Sea To The West* Nicholson gives it Wigan to the last, and in the title poem, a moving farewell, he thinks of the times he has looked at the sunset and says:

> Yet in that final stare when I
> (Five times, perhaps, fifteen)
> Creak protesting away –
> The sea to the west,
> The land darkening –
> Let my eyes at the last be blinded
> Not by the dark
> But by dazzle.

These closing lines are now on his tombstone (facing west) in Millom churchyard.*

Nicholson himself wrote about many other writers and poets, but never more perceptively than about William Cowper, that gifted English Christian provincial poet who spent so much of his life in the small town of Olney and who could write so entertainingly about his sofa. It was as early as 1951 that Norman Nicholson wrote his critical biography of Cowper and so he perhaps did not realize how doubly appropriate was its final sentence:

> In his precarious pilgrimage he looked at the few feet of grass about him, at the creatures he saw, or the fireside he knew, with a love wide enough to include all Nature and all his fellow-men, and with the sharp tenderness of a long Good-bye.

---

* On the headstone the word 'our' has been substituted for the word 'my'.

SELECTED POEMS

(1943)

Corregidor

Over this island breaks the war
Like the Pacific pounding on the shore,
Like the shingle shovelled and hurled at the bare
Cliff, like the buffet and blow and shock
Of the heavy fist of the sea on the rock.
Above the crags the eagle flies
And looks the sun straight in the eyes.

Dawn after dawn the broken foam
Falls back, the jellyfish and the yellow scum,
But the octopus coils round the trunk of the palm.
The eagle fights as the waters rise,
Tears at the tentacles, the squids and the stinging rays,
And into the spray his body flings
Till the salt like acid burns his wings.

He stares across the ocean, listens to the drone
Of the spinning world where the crying islands shine:
Guam, Hawaii, Midway, Solomon.
And whether the winds of tomorrow find
Him clinging to the ledge or on the long reef drowned,
All wings that to this headland flock
Shall see an eagle's talons blazoned on the rock.

[3]

Carol For Holy Innocents' Day

The cat was let out of the bag by an angel
  Who warned them and planned their get-away,
And told how Herod would make holy with death
  The day that a birth made a holy day.

Herod's men were searching the backalleys,
  They did not see the refugees go,
Nor how when the child's hands fluttered like sparrow
  His fingers blessed the casual snow.

The boy saw sand white as snow in the desert,
  And watched it thaw to husks of corn;
And perhaps his merchant uncle showed him
  The first white blossoms of the Glastonbury thorn.

We have hurried the children from a german Herod,
  Whose bombs stretch further than a city's roofs;
We have brought them westward across the Pennines
  To where the sea like a squadron moves.

They will see the bracken retard and turn rusty,
  And new fronds like clock-springs coil into gear;
Many times they will watch the sea's renewal,
  And oftener than we know the renewal of the year.

In farms among the hills and in small mining towns
  Safe the umartyred innocents lie;
But on the frozen cradle of Europe
  The infant Jesus is left to die.

Before I Was Born

Before I was born the sea was a waste of rocks;
The grass was dry as raffia on the hills;
Bramble and dogrose wired the woods and walls,
With blossoms hard as coral on their stalks;
Trees held their branches stiff as a reindeer's horn
In the dead land, before I was born.

Empty hides, then, roared to the flat moon;
Clay, fledged with feathers, flew in the sky;
Bones, slated with scales, swam in the sea;
The creatures knew no joy in sun or rain;
There was no festival for the miraculous corn
In the thankless land, before I was born.

Before I was born a clock ticked in the skull,
Laughter was clatter of the cruel spring;
There was no catechism of right or wrong,
No hope of heaven and no fear of hell;
There was no devil's halo in a crown of thorn
In the undamned land, before I was born.

Before I was born the sky was as black as ink,
The steeples spiked towards the hollow clouds,
The frantic churchbells yelled their harsh tirades,
The sun, if there were a sun, was a conjuring trick
Then was I no one, ears were blocked, eyes torn –
But I am Nicodemus now I'm born.

Love Was There in Eden

Love was there in Eden
Under the Sunday-school banners
Of the bright trees, laden
With fruit and birds and words of God,
But Love lay in the mud,
Learned a snake's manners,
With a snake's tongue taught.
Aprons of leaf,
And a retrospect grief,
To Eden, Love brought.

The girl whose ears were deaf
To a snake's voice, felt
Love rise in her breast
As the loved one knelt.
But to kneel was not enough,
And the love unsucked
Like milk turned sour,
Filled the veins with pain,
Gave the flesh no rest,
Till the limbs which loved before
Feared to love again.

And that tall proud woman
With heart and skeleton
Stiff as a crucifix
To nail her love on,
Had once a tree's charms,
As with sap of young oaks,
As with rowan's grace,
Before the wooden arms
Were spliced with her love's embrace.

But the man whose wish
Before the birds were gone
Was to know all women
In loving one,
Seeks now the love
Of the fisherman for the fish,
That he may praise the Unfallen
In singing the Fall,
And know one woman
In loving all.

FIVE RIVERS

(1944)

Five Rivers

Southward from Whitehaven, where cliffs of coal
Slant like shale to the low black mole,
The railway canters along the curving shore
Over five rivers, which slowly pour
On the steps of the shingle where the grey gulls bask
EHEN and CALDER, IRT and MITE and ESK.

The EHEN twists and flicks its fin
Red as rhubarb beneath the grey skin,
For its veins are stained with the blood of the ore
Of the mines of Egremont and Cleator Moor.
Here drill and navvy break the stone
And hack the living earth to the bone;
Blood spurts like water from the stricken rock.
Seeps into drain and gully and trickles to the beck.
Green herringbones of watercresses ride
On the tilt and tug of the red tide;
Bladderwrack, thrift and salty turf
Crust over cobbles at the edge of the pink surf.

The introspective CALDER hums to the pebbles
A memory of plainsong and choirboys' trebles,
Of collect and introit, creed and antiphon,
Of cistercians in the abbey of blood-red stone,
Where now tarpaulin and sheet lead shield
Groined roof and cloister and stoup from the wild
Weather of time, and the wall ferns spread
Where once the praying lamp hung before the holy bread.

The IRT comes from Wastdale, the land of the screes,
Of bracken up to your waist and ham-and-egg teas,
Of men who remember Will Ritson, the biggest liar
That ever lived, who sit by the fire
And laugh their inherited laughs at the talk
Of hounds with wings of eagles sniffing the lake.

The mite, the tyke, lollops along
Like a blue-haired collie with a dribbling tongue,
The children's plaything as they ride the toy train
That runs beneath the rocks in a hawthorn lane,
Where dog-daisy, dogrose and stiff dog-grass
Bark at the wheels as the whistling truckloads pass.

But the ESK comes from the narrowest dale
Where statesmen meet at the Woolpack for a glass of ale
And a crack about herdwicks or a cure for the tick
And how some fool has broken his neck on the rock.
The esk knows the stonechat and the parsley fern
And breaks like a bottle at every turn,
And bursts on the boulders and froths like beer,
Runs solid as glass and green and clear,
Till it mixes with MITE and IRT in the marsh,
Where roman cement and arches teach
Of the galleys that came to Ravenglass
Bearing the invaders with helmets of brass.
Where the plover creaks and the curlew whines,
The rivers ferret among the dunes,
Till the channels burst through a gap in the sand
Like a three-pronged pitchfork jabbed in the flank of the land.

Brown clouds are blown against the bright fells
Like Celtic psalms from drowned western isles.
The slow rain falls like memory
And floods the becks and flows to the sea,
And there on the coast of Cumberland mingle
The fresh and the salt, the cinders and the shingle.

Egremont

November sunlight floats and falls
Like soapsuds on the castle walls.
Where broken groins are slanted west
The bubbles touch the stone and burst,
And the moist shadows dribble down
And slime the sandy red with brown.

Here the hawkweed still contrives
Sustenance for mouse-ear leaves;
On fallen lintels groundsel rubs
Its heads of seed like lather-blobs;
And ragwort's stubborn flowers hold
Trayfuls of their pinchbeck gold.

Rain erases the written stone;
Boss and dog-tooth now are gone;
But yet the sandstone vaults and walls
Are scutcheoned with heraldic tales,
Of when Picts crossed the Roman fosse
And foraged down from Solway Moss.

Still the moated dungeons hide
Legends of poverty and pride,
And murdered skulls are stuffed with lore
Of pillage, plunder, famine, fear,
And dirk has carved upon the bone:
'Blood will not show on the red stone'.

The damp autumnal sunlight drips
On chimneys, pit-shafts, rubble-tips.
Centuries of feudal weight
Have made men stoop towards their feet.
They climb no rocks nor stare around,
But dig their castles in the ground.

Castles in the red ore made
Are buttressed, tunnelled, turretted,
And like a moat turned inside out
The pit-heaps trap the sieging light,
With lantern-flints the miners spark
And gouge their windows to the dark.

Here in the hollows the men store,
Rich as rubies, the red ore;
And rock and bones are broken both
When the stone spine is theft from earth.
The crime defiles like a red mud
The ore, the sandstone, and the blood.

But the robbed earth will claim its own
And break the mines and castles down
When Gabriel from heaven sent
Blows the Horn of Egremont,
Tabulates the tenants' needs
And reassumes the title-deeds.

According to tradition the Horn of Egremont can be blown only by the rightful
owner of the castle. This is the theme of a poem by William Wordsworth.

Cleator Moor

From one shaft at Cleator Moor
They mined for coal and iron ore.
This harvest below ground could show
Black and red currants on one tree.

In furnaces they burnt the coal,
The ore was smelted into steel,
And railway lines from end to end
Corseted the bulging land.

Pylons sprouted on the fells,
Stakes were driven in like nails,
And the ploughed fields of Devonshire
Were sliced with the steel of Cleator Moor.

The land waxed fat and greedy too,
It would not share the fruits it grew,
And coal and ore, as sloe and plum,
Lay black and red for jamming time.

The pylons rusted on the fells,
The gutters leaked beside the walls,
And women searched the ebb-tide tracks
For knobs of coal or broken sticks.

But now the pits are wick with men,
Digging like dogs dig for a bone:
For food and life *we* dig the earth-
In Cleator Moor they dig for death.

Every waggon of cold coal
Is fire to drive a turbine wheel;
Every knuckle of soft ore
A bullet in a soldier's ear.

The miner at the rockface stands,
With his segged and bleeding hands
Heaps on his head the fiery coal,
And feels the iron in his soul.

Whitehaven

In this town the dawn is late.
For suburbs like a waking beast
Hoist their backbones to the east,
And pitheaps at the seaward gate
Build barricades against the light.
Deep as trenches streets are dug
Beneath entanglements of fog,
And dull and stupid the tide lies
Within the harbour's lobster claws.
Curlews wheel on the north wind,
Their bills still moist with Solway sand,
And waves slide up from the wide bays
With rumours of the Hebrides.
But anchored to the jetty stones
Bladderwrack gnaws at the town's bones;
Barnacle, cockle, crab and mussel
Suck at the pier's decaying gristle;
And limpet keeps its tongue and dream
Riveted to an inch of home.
At the Atlantic's dying edge
The harbour now prepares for siege.
The mole intimidates the sea,
The bastions of the colliery
Are battlemented like a fort –
This is the last invasion port.

Not at Hastings, Medway, Skye,
But here on rock of Cumberland
Foreign invader last made stand.
In April 1778
Came John Paul Jones, the Yankee-Scot,
Apprentice from Kirkcudbrightshire,
Who learned his trade by box on ear,
Saw a wench whipped at Market Cross,
And spitting gold, without a toss
Of pence for publican or lover,
Sailed to the New World in a slaver.
He came at spring tide from the west,
The setting sun behind his mast;
His sails like gulls of flame that fell
On the scared ships behind the mole,
And scattered feathered fire on quays
And eighteenth-century warehouses.
Many a joiner's broken head
Paid for the knocks a 'prentice had,
And ashes of the harbour inns
Did penance for the landlord's sins.

This is the time the walls remember.
The lintels crack it with the street,
And pavements teach to passing feet,
And strangers feel within their veins
The cold suspicion of the stones.
Every man and woman born
In shade of this beleaguered town
Bargains brain and blood and thew
To keep the world from breaking through.

But the town's fort will fall at last
When the sea rams and bursts the mole,
And the mines vomit up their coal,
And dawn upon the breaking slate
Drops in an avalanche of light;
When Gabriel, the brigand, guides
His fiery frigate down the clouds,
Tears up the lighthouse in his hand
And waves it like a burning brand
Before the pennon, nailed to mast,
The Jolly Roger of the Blest –
Skull of Adam, Cross of Christ.
The merchants then will sell the town
To make their bartered souls their own,
Hoist high their white flag in the sky
And yield to heaven's piracy.

St Bees

St Bega's spire beneath the hill
Chips the night's blue window-sill;
St Bega's Head beyond the bay
Buttresses a stained-glass sky.

Above the holy thoroughfares
Move intelligent new stars.
Red and green and white reveal
A constellation framed by steel,
That follows no deductive course
But tests and tries the universe.
With a man's hands and eyes it goes,
Empiric as a spaniel's nose.

The Home-Guards by the railway-line
Listen to the nearing plane,
Hide torches to conserve the night
And curse the moon that gives them light.
They long for nights as dark as mire
When sea is one with shale and shore,
When the black wind from the cold fell
Freezes their bones and the foe's oil.
They cheer the gale that rips out summer's
Remnant leaves and foreign bombers,
And welcome blizzard, hail and storm
That keep their starving courage warm.

Bega, in answer to whose prayer
The meek snow fell at midsummer,
Gazes from the haloed rocks
At this unprayed-for paradox.

Eskmeals 1943

The fat tide thrusts its hand
High among the long ribs of the land;
The fields are under the waves;
Road and riverside and fence are gone,
And the bridges stand
Sheer out of the flat water, and telephone wires
Run like a handrail along the edges of stone piers.

The whin bushes push above the tide
Like rocks grown over with thorny weed
And barnacled with yellow eyes.
The February sun is tight and pale as skin
On hazels and willows by the slaty shore,
Where the skyline lifts through fir and chestnut trees
To snowy mountains chalked on the grey skies.

The train crosses the viaduct and leaves
A caterpillar of smoke along the waves.
It brings the children home from school –
The little girl with love unbudded beneath her skin,
The lad with electricity latent in his gloves.
What will they see when the mountains melt in rain,
And the receded water lets the meadows live again?

To the River Duddon

I wonder, Duddon, if you still remember
An oldish man with a nose like a pony's nose,
Broad bones, legs long and lean but strong enough
To carry him over Hardknott at seventy years of age.
He came to you first as a boy with a fishing-rod
And a hunk of Ann Tyson's bread and cheese in his pocket,
Walking from Hawkshead across Walna Scar;
Then as a middle-aged Rydal landlord,
With a doting sister and a pension on the civil list,
Who left his verses gummed to your rocks like lichen,
The dry and yellow edges of a once-green spring.
He made a guide-book for you, from your source
There where you bubble through the moss on Wrynose
(Among the ribs of bald and bony fells
With screes scratched in the turf like grey scabs),
And twist and slither under humpbacked bridges –
Built like a child's house from odds and ends
Of stones that lie about the mountain side –
Past Cockley Beck Farm and on to Birk's Bridge,
Where the rocks stride about like legs in armour,
And the steel birches buckle and bounce in the wind
With a crinkle of silver foil in the crisp of the leaves;
On then to Seathwaite, where like a steam-navvy
You shovel and slash your way through the gorge
By Wallabarrow Crag, broader now
From becks that flow out of black upland tarns
Or ooze through golden saxifrage and the roots of rowans;
Next Ulpha, where a stone dropped from the bridge
Swims like a tadpole down thirty feet of water

Between steep skirting-boards of rock; and thence
You dribble into lower Dunnerdale
Through wet woods and wood-soil and woodland flowers,
Tutson, the St. John's-wort with a single yellow bead,
Marsh marigold, creeping jenny and daffodils;
Here from hazel islands in the late spring
The catkins fall and ride along the stream
Like little yellow weasels, and the soil is loosed
From bulbs of the white lily that smells of garlic,
And dippers rock up and down on rubber legs,
And long-tailed tits are flung through the air like darts;
By Foxfield now you taste the salt in your mouth,
And thrift mingles with the turf, and the heron stands
Watching the wagtails. Wordsworth wrote:
'Remote from every taint of sordid industry'.
But you and I know better, Duddon lass.
For I, who've lived for nearly thirty years
Upon your shore, have seen the slagbanks slant
Like screes sheer into the sand, and seen the tide
Purple with ore back up the muddy gullies
And wiped the sinter dust from the farmyard damsons.
A hundred years of floods and rain and wind
Have washed your rocks clear of his words again,
Many of them half-forgotten, brimming the Irish Sea,
But that which Wordsworth knew, even the old man
When poetry had failed like desire, was something
I have yet to learn, and you, Duddon,
Have learned and re-learned to forget and forget again.
Not the radical, the poet and heretic,
To whom the water-forces shouted and the fells
Were like a blackboard for the scrawls of God,
But the old man, inarticulate and humble,
Knew that eternity flows in a mountain beck –

The long cord of the water, the shepherd's numerals
That run upstream, through the singing decades of dialect.
He knew, beneath mutation of year and season,
Flood and drought, frost and fire and thunder,
The frothy blossom on the rowan and the reddening of the
  berries,
The silt, the sand, the slagbanks and the shingle,
And the wild catastrophes of the breaking mountains,
There stands the base and root of the living rock,
Thirty thousand feet of solid Cumberland.

Cockley Moor, Dockray, Penrith

Outside, the cubist fells are drawn again
Beneath the light that speaks extempore;
The fur of bracken thickens in the rain
And wrinkles shift upon the scurfy scree.

Inside, like tiles the poet's pleasures lie,
Square laid on circle, circle laid on square,
And pencilled angles of eternity
Are calculated on the doubled stair.

Outside, the curlew gargles through the mist,
The mountain pansies shut up shop and fade,
The wheatear chisels with his crystal fist,
And day on day like stone on stone is laid.

Inside, are cows on canvas, painted bloom
Fresh as a girl's thin fingers burst to flower,
Bright leaves that do not fall, but fence the room
With the arrested growth of a June hour.

The curving cloud embellishes the sky,
The geometric rain slants to the corn;
Inside, a man remembers he must die,
Outside, a stone forgets that it was born.

Bombing Practice

In the long estuary now the water
At the top and turn of the tide
Is quiet as a mountain tarn,
Smooth and dull as pewter,
Pale as the mauve sea-aster
In the turf of the gutter-side.

The fells are purple and blurred in the haze above the marshes;
The gulls float like bubbles.
Plovers band together with white bellies
Square into the wind;
A curlew flies crying along the gullies;
A faint rainbow of oil is clogged in the thin rushes.

The swinging aeroplane drops seed through the air
Plumb into the water, where slowly it grows
Boles of smoke and trees
Of swelling and ballooning leafage,
Silver as willows
Or white as a blossoming pear.

The trees float seaward, spreading and filling like sails,
And the smoke mingles with the sea-mist when
The breeze shreds it. And the curlew sadly cries
That things so beautiful as these
Shall fall through nights of winter gales
And plant their germs of pain in the limbs of men.

South Cumberland, 10 May 1943

The fat flakes fall
In parachute invasion from the yellow sky.
The streets are quiet and surprised; the snow
Clutters the roofs with a wet crust, but no
Dry harbour is found on soil or wall.

In the town
The fledgling sparrows are puzzled and take fright;
The weedy hair of the slagbank in an hour turns white.
Flakes fill the tulips in backyard plots;
The chimneys snow upward and the snow smokes down.

Beyond the fells
Dawn lumbers up, and the peaks are white through the mist.
The young bracken is buttoned with snow; the knobs
Of crabapple trees are in bloom again, and blobs
Hang on the nettles like canterbury bells.

This job is mine
And everyone's: to force our blood into the bitter day.
The hawthorn scorched and blasted by the flames of the wind
On the sheltered side greens out a dogged spray –
And this is our example, our duty and our sign.

South Cumberland, 16 May 1943

The sun has set
Behind Black Combe and the lower hills,
But northward in the sky the fells
Like gilded galleons on a sea of shadow
Float sunlit yet.

The liquid light
Soaks into the dry motes of the air,
Bright and moist until the flood of dawn;
Shoals of swifts round the market tower
Swim with fish-like flight.

Six days ago
The fells were limed with snow; the starlings on the chimney
    pots
Shook the falling flakes off their tin feathers.
May gives a sample of four seasons' weathers
For a week on show.

Coastal Journey

A wet wind blows the waves across the sunset;
There is no more sea nor sky.
And the train halts where the railway line
Twists among the misty shifting sand,
Neither land nor estuary,
Neither wet nor dry.

In the blue dusk of the empty carriage
There is no more here nor there,
No more you nor me.
Green like a burning apple
The signal hangs in the pines beside the shore
And shines All Clear.

There is no more night nor evening;
No more now nor then.
There is only us and everywhere and always.
The train moves off again,
And the sandy pinetrees bend
Under the dark green berries of the rain.

Song

For M.

At the sea's kerb, at the wide
Turn of the dune
The burnet rose
Grows in its green
Ravel of leaves like seaweed,
White as bare flesh
When the bright June sun
Flows in on the flush of the tide.

There my hopes
Bloom like a harebell,
Of laughter along the shingle,
Bare arms on the sand,
A cranesbill in a girl's hair,
Of the one kiss found
Whorled like a shell
In the tangle of the sea's frayed ropes.

And now frost closes
On the blown bloom,
And the frozen foam
Lies like salt on the mosses,
And the windy sand
Flings its dry rain
On the dune where my dream
Is rooted deep as the roses.

Songs of the Island

Westward from Britain the souls embark,
Leaving the dark land, leaving the smoke
Of charcoal woods, the shadow of rock and oak;

Leaving the ring of stones on the moor,
Leaving St Patrick's trinity-flower,
And the elder haunted by the blood it bore.

Westward the islands lie like sleeping gulls,
The clouds like islands. The rain falls,
The mist rises, as the boat sails,

Sails, with a ballast of souls, between
The islands in the shining rain,
Where the flying foam reflects the sun.

Eyes on the prow discover the sky,
And the tides teach new tongues to the sea,
And the compass points in more than one way.

The known land is forgotten; the name
Of the unknown island is a charm,
And the sea flows above the drowned bones of time.

II

Still we climb, higher we climb,
Through the bracken in the dark combe,
Through the bilberries and the wild thyme,

Through the mist, through the rain,
Above the clouds, above the tarn,
Following the track towards the remembered cairn.

There, a shelduck's flight from the fells,
Is the boundary between the owl's house and the gull's,
The sand and shingle and broken shells.

There, westward, there, stretches the sea,
Beyond the bare shore, beyond the promontory,
Cloud-like the water beneath a watery sky.

Still we climb, and higher,
Remembering the horizon, staring far,
For there, if the mist shifts, if the sky lifts, there,

There, as we remember it, there, lies,
As we hoped for it, under westward skies,
As we dreamed of it, the island beyond the light of our eyes.

Maiden's Song

(A Song of the Island)

From here the ships go out one by one,
As dawn lifts on the lilt of the tide they are gone,
Leaving the warehouses and wharves of stone.

Northward the stone breaks through the shore-line fog,
Making a wall for the turnip field, a shelter for the shepherd's
    dog,
A nesting ledge for the puffin and the shag.

Daily I watch the ships
Topple beyond the horizon where the sunset dips,
Daily I hear the sea whisper with wet lips.

The ships sail to the island and never come back,
Only a broken barrel drifts against the rock,
Only a spar or a sailor's fingers tangled in the wrack.

Daily at the shingle's edge I gather wood,
And pick the sea-coal from bladders of salty weed,
Daily I feel the tug of the tide in my blood;

Yet still I remain when the ships and the gulls are gone,
Feeling the rock beneath my ankles, feeling the bone
Spliced in the iron roots of the dead stone.

For the Grieg Centenary

The fells are jagged in the shining air; the wind
Sharpens itself like a knife on the rough edges:
The sky is blue as ice, and clouds from the sea
    Splinter above the land
And drive against the rocks in thin steel wedges.

This of all England is the place to remember Grieg:
Here where the Norsemen foraged down the dales,
Crossing the sea with the migrant redwing,
    Thieving heifer and yow and teg,
Leaving their names scotched on the flanks of the hills.

Leaving also the crackling northern tongues,
The dialect crisp with the click of the wind
In the thorns of a wintry dyke,
    So that Solvieg sings
In the words which bind the homes of Cumberland.

Therefore let Solvieg sing in the western dales
When the frost is on the pikes, and the raven builds again
Its nest in February; let Crinkle Crags
    Be thumped by the humpbacked trolls,
And the voice of Grieg ring loud through the sound of the sea
    and the rain.

Askam Unvisited

All through the summer I planned to visit Askam. Now
Dusk falls before the smoke rises from the slate,
Leaves curl up like caterpillars on the bough

Of the sycamores by the public library, dahlias are dark and
  wet,
Children shout again in the playground of the school,
Mauve toadstools knuckle the bowling green. And yet

Askam remains an intention and a goal,
Or perhaps a sin of omission, an opportunity missed,
A place marked on a map that hands let fall

Out of the carriage window or into the fire, a letter lost
In the post. But Askam is real enough and clear to be seen
Across the estuary, a mile and a half at most,

Not twenty miles by road nor twenty minutes in the train –
Its chimney stacks that never smoke; and the steep little hills
Of rubble overgrown with weed; grey slagbanks that rear
  between

The low yellow dunes and the high green fells;
The long rows of houses, where unexpected windows glow
Like mica when the sunset takes to its heels.

The greater commandments I readily know,
Not to kill, nor steal, nor love incontinently –
These have not always to be thought of. But the lightning
  scores no

Signposts in stone beside the choices that lie
Like a spreading maze before me – whether to go or stay,
Whether to speak or be silent, whether to raise an eye

To an eye, a hand to a hand, turn this or that way.
Among these I walk haphazard, like a bird pecking crumbs,
Aware of the wild importance of each moment, though

Unaware of the meaning of the moment when it comes.
So let Askam remain, at least for a while,
Secure and secret as the lucky dip of dreams –

The wader on the marsh, the bugloss on the sands, the half-
  acknowledged smile
From a girl on a bicycle, let these be bright as berries.
Without their trail of consequence pointing to a final trial.

Askam Visited

Seventy or eighty years ago and more
Before the days of the railway, travellers crossed the sands
On horseback or in carts, starting from this shore

To dig for mud and gold in Cumberland
And found the iron town which is my home.
The land was eager then for settlers, opened heart and hand

To men from Wales and Ireland, strange in name
And cult and dialect. Now no more it hopes
For colonizing voices – every mine and farm

Spikes the intruder's path with stakes like props
For clothes-lines in a huge deserted square. The sky is dull.
From steep clay dunes the water drops

And dribbles like the Knaresborough Dripping Well.
The sand is red with ore, and yellow flowers
Grow in the red sand: dandelion and tormentil. Small

Pink cranesbills too are there, and hemlock storksbill bears
Its shiny button above a scuffle of grimy leaves.
The curlews whinney on the marsh. The slagbank rears

Itself above the shore, and juts into the waves
Of sand like a harbour mole. Half-silted-up and overgrown
    with weed,
Hairy with horse-tails, it almost moves,

Romantic, ugly, grey and horrid, not dead
Enough to be forgotten, nor living enough to be damned. All
This is limbo. Yet children with bucket and spade

Build irrigations in the sand, and a little girl
Thrusts up her voice like grass through a concrete floor.
In the time when the slag is only a memorial

Of a haematite dream, and the sky is bright and clear,
The sea and the hope and the children will be new with the
   light and the year.

Wales

Walking on the step of the shingle, here
Where the curlew follows the scallop of bay
And halts and prods the sand,
Looking beyond the cormorant's thoroughfare.
Beyond the drift and dip of the sea,
I saw the hills of Wales like stone clouds stand.

The sea flowed round them and the sky
Flowed under, and the floating peaks
Were frozen high in air;
I was a child then, and the winters blew
Mist across the skyline and spray against the rocks,
But blew open that window into Wales no more.

This year as a neighbour I looked at Wales;
Saw the sun on the rocks and the wind in the bracken,
And the telegraph poles like a boundary fence
Straddle the combe between the hills,
And westward from England and the Wrekin
Saw shadows of clouds advance.

But the sun was hot on the limbs, the turf on the heels,
The berries were fat as grapes, and the way
Bent back on the Shropshire side of the border –
I walked no nearer Wales,
But returned to wait by the former sea,
Aware that the mist will never lift to order.

Shrewsbury

For E. A. B.

The spires spike the morning mists.
Oh holy saints,
Alkmund, Julian, Chad,
Remember me in your plaints,
Turn the wheels of prayer with your practised wrists.

Alkmund, Julian, Chad,
When the burghers rode to the ford,
When the Severn washed the blood off the ragwort stems.
You suffered for the Lord,
You remembered the sins of the living and the dead.

The roofs are red in the sun,
Bright and jagged as broken glass;
The domes are busy with birds;
In the steel sickle of the river lies,
Pale beneath plantagenet mists, the unremembering town.

September leaves are blown against the churchyard wall.
Alkmund, Julian, Chad,
Stiff as steeples in prayer
Above the stone insignia of your trade,
Remember me when the roofs are broken and the spires fall.

September in Shropshire

Now as I travel along the northern marshes
To a winter of slag and frozen mountains
I remember chiefly an undated evening
Standing at a window that looked across to Wales –
The shadows hanging like bats in the Virginia creeper,
Tomatoes redder than the brick they grew against,
The dunce-caps of convolvulus lying on the coke,
It seemed then that the pith and pride of England
Was ripening like a peach upon the stable wall,
With none to gather it, none to treasure it,
For the labourer's hands were bound or cut from the wrist.
There was much else also ready to be remembered –
The September sun as hot as a kiss of parting,
The autumn songs of the chiffchaff and the chaffinch,
The herald moth like a withered leaf, the blue
Earrings of bilberries on the tiny lobes of the leaves.
The comic victorian house,
Where Mrs. Radcliffe haunts the hearth like a downdraught,
I therefore leave to you who already have so much,
Holding in your arms the wind that blows from Wales
And sings like a wren in the frosty trees,
Holding the sunlight and the wild birds' fruit,
Elderberry, cranberry, crabapple, hip and sloe,
Holding the healed and healthy limbs of children,
Laughing at the future in four acres of beans and chickens.
You know so much that is half-forgotten now –
The nudge of the catkin beneath the drying leaf,
The spring intentions of the swallow, the fantastic
Sting of love in the blood, the brutal wooing of God.

And so I leave you
To hoard the bright pods of a dying summer
In the brown and poignant winter of this war.

For Hokey and Henrietta

Now it is midsummer and the long sun shines
At my bedtime as it does at yours,
And, however early you wake, the yellow lines

Of the sun are lying like straw on the bedroom chairs,
And there are bees and creatures without names,
And, if you remember to look, there are always flowers.

Winter is a name for strange forgotten times,
Times as distant as bananas, when
The frost in the wind was a boxer, and goodnight games

Stalked round the fire like gypsies in caravan.
But winter will be real when laburnum turns to fibre
And the windows are black and the stories bright again.

Hokey, of course, will be polite to October,
Introduce it to his mother and show no surprise,
And Henrietta will hug it like a new neighbour.

In a world where worms are friends, and visiting eyes
Look for camels in the kitchen or under the stairs,
Winter will fall as gently as the snow on the trees.

What more can you learn to ask for in your prayers,
Than years unpredicted as weather, and days
Adventurous as a lobby full of bears?

For Anne and Alison

The night is clear now the rain is gone; the stars
Lie in yellow splinters on the wet road
Among the blurred spilled headlights of passing cars.

Tonight I will not remember the day's dark cloud
That booms beyond the mountains, nor think of the wind
That tomorrow may blow the thunder back to our broad

And individualistic valleys. Here the land
Is still unblackened by war; here the corn
Is planted at the curve of the year. So I hold in mind

The baby soon to be born or already born,
Even if never to be known by me – for as Christ's death
Gave life to the living and made the young dead turn

Like a waking child, so this and every birth
Repudiates all dying on the earth.

Rockferns

On quarry walls the spleenwort spreads
Its green zipfasteners and black threads,
And pinches tight its unfurled purses
In every crevice with the cresses,
As if a blast of dynamite
Had spattered it upon the slate
That where the bluestone spine was broken
Spores might penetrate and quicken.
For in the fractures of the rock
Roots dig further than a pick,
As, though the sinews may not feel it,
The worm probes deeper than the bullet.
When this pen is dropped, my hand
May thrust up in a buckler frond,
And then my crushed and calcined bones
Prove better soil than arid stones.
Why need I fear the bursting bomb
Or whatsoever death should come,
If brains and bowels be cast forth
Splintered to spleenwort on the earth?
And if a subtler part may cruise
Twice round the sun and Betelgeuse,
My soul shall detonate on high
And plant itself in cracks of sky.

The Blackberry

Between the railway and the mine,
Brambles are in fruit again.
 Their little nigger fists they clench,
 And hold the branches in a clinch.
Waggons of ore are shunted past,
And spray the berries with red dust,
 Which dulls the bright mahogany
 Like purple sawdust clogged and dry.
But when the housewife, wind-and-rain,
Rubs the berry spick and span,
 Compound it gleams like a fly's eye,
 And every ball reflects the sky.
There the world's repeated like
Coupons in a ration book;
 There the tall curved chimneys spread
 Purple smoke on purple cloud.
Grant us to know that hours rushed by
Are photographed upon God's eye;
 That life and leaf are both preserved
 In gelatine of Jesus' blood.
And grant to us the sense to feel
The large condensed within the small;
 Wash clear our eyes that we may see
 The sky within the blackberry.

Horsetails

Now the first green scud of spring
   Blows through the furrow,
And by the rusty iron rails
   Horsetails grow.

Like little lighthouses they stand
   Above brown waves of plough,
And scatter yellow, sandy spores
   Here and now;

Waiting not for summer when
   The brushy branches rise,
And like green tails of shetland ponies
   Swish at the skies;

Anxious to get the job of seeding
   Over and forgot –
Then no need to worry whether
   Summer comes or not.

Waiting for Spring 1943

A grey wind blows
Through the woods, and the birches are bare,
And the hazel crooks its catkins tight as a starling's claws;
But out in the fields where the dyker hacks the branches
Of purple willow and elder and wrenches
The trunks square to the run of the hedge, there
The yellow lamb's-tails dangle in the frosty air.

So also we
On the perimeter and fringe of war,
Open to the sunlight and the wind from the western sea,
Wounded by the knife of winter, still
Feel the bright blood rise to bear
White and daring blossoms, fledged before
The seabirds leave the ploughland or the snow leaves the fell.

Let us not forget
Those in whom autumn dug deep furrows of pain,
Those to whom winter has been the kindliest season yet,
The snow their only eiderdown, the frost
Their only morphia; they will not greet again
The sap that stings in the bone, nor the bird on the nest
That hatches globes of suffering in the probing rain.

Blood flows back
Into the frozen hand with pain,
And children whimper as the wind flogs them again awake.
To those defeated by the winter's cold
Spring is a terrible season, atonement not to be told
To us in our temperate valleys, who scarcely have begun
To feel the anger of love beneath the conquering sun.

Stalingrad: 1942

The broken sandstone slabs litter the shore
Like gingerbread; the shingle, pink and grey,
Slants to the runnels of the rocky floor
Where seaweed greens the red edge of the sea.

The tide rides up from Ireland, and a peel
Of sun curls round the axles of the waves;
The rough tongue of the water like the steel
Tongue of a limpet strops the kerb of caves.

Stalingrad now has stood the flood of fire,
Three moons of tide, for more than eighty days;
And this for more than eighty hundred year
Has borne the barrage of the western seas.

Whatever names wash over Stalingrad,
Or salt corrodes its stone, or torrents shock
Its cliffs, the city will not change, though blood
Settle like ore in the red veins of rock.

The Evacuees

Four years ago
They came to this little town
Carrying their bundles – women who did not know
Where the sky would lie when their babies were born, mothers
With children, children with sisters and brothers,
Children with schoolmates, and frightened children alone.
They saw the strangers at the station, the sea-mist on the hill,
In the windless waiting days when the walls of Poland fell.

Winter came
And the wind did not rise; the sky
Withheld its threat of thunderbolt or bomb.
The women were lonely. Thoughts began to bend
To Northumbrian voices high as a seagull's cry,
To the smell of the North Sea in the streets, the foggy air,
The fish-shops and the neighbours. The tide of fear
Flowed back, leaving weary empty sand.

The women returned
To the Tyneside husbands and the Tyneside coal,
And most of the children followed. Others stayed and learned
The Cumberland vowels, took strangers for their friends,
Went home for holidays at first, then not at all,
Accepted in the aisle the bishop's hands,
Won scholarships and badges, and were known
One with the indigenous children of the town.

Four years ago
They came, and in four childhood years
The memory shrivels and the muscles grow.
The little girl who wept on the platform then
Now feels her body blossom like the trees,
Discovers tennis, poetry and flowers,
And under the dripping larches in the rain
Knows the first experiment of a kiss.

Will they rest,
Will they be contented, these
Fledglings oi a cuckoo's egg reared in a stranger's nest?
Born of one people, with another bred,
Will they return to their parents again, or choose
The foster-home, or seek the unrented road?
Grant that in the future they may find
A rock on which to build a house for heart and mind.

For St James, 1943

The last clinkers of sunset are strewn on the hill;
The mist is blown about the town like smoke.
Girls stand in the street in the brown dusk
Talking to soldiers, and the swifts still
Wire their screaming spirals round the market clock.

Now the foretelling of baptism holds no fear;
Now we accept the water like the rain;
Now we are able to take the cup.
The purple evening is like holy wine;
We drink in grace and feel the spirit near.

But what of those to whom the bright winds bring
Baptismal brands already, those on whom the sun
Fires bullets, and acid rains from clouds,
Those whose desperate muscles thrust along
A tight clot of faith in the thin dry vein?

Yet this evening's quiet does not deceive:
The quiet is what endures. The swifts fly higher
Through the drifting ash of the last light
Into the nights of the future. And all we now believe
Still will be true when the sky is wild with fire.

The Burning Bush

When Moses, musing in the desert, found
The thorn bush spiking up from the hot ground,
And saw the branches, on a sudden, bear
The crackling yellow barberries of fire,

He searched his learning and imagination
For any logical, neat explanation,
And turned to go, but turned again and stayed
And faced the fire and knew it for his God.

I too have seen the briar alight like coal,
The love that burns, the flesh that's ever whole,
And many times have turned and left it there,
Saying: 'It's prophecy – but metaphor.'

But stinging tongues like John the Baptist shout:
'That this is metaphor is no way out.
It's dogma too, or you make God a liar;
The bush is still a bush, and fire is fire.'

Babylon

The wind was bright when we left the trading isles,
The sun was keen as a western gale; our keel
Cut like a saw the rolling logs of the sea.
Porpoise bounced in the waves' blue shavings,
And gulls followed our decks as they follow a plough.
We were stuffed with cargo below, tight as a drum:
Bales of cotton and linen and spiderweb silk,
And wool in the fleece, soaking with oil and water,
And grain, the finest of a fortunate harvest,
And butter down in the ice-box, packed into barrels,
And the island fruits, pomegranates, melons, bananas,
And coconuts, tapioca, spice.
As we swung into the straits a landward fog rose up
And rubbed out the stars. We hung off-shore a while,
Missing the navigation lights, while unseen
Mountains boomed and thundered, and stars shot through the
      fog,
And the water was alive with fiery fishes –
Such sights we were accustomed to in the tropic seas
But not in the estuary. We waited for dawn
And the mist to rise. Dawn came and the mist was there,
And the sun sprang out of the sea, and we saw that the mist
      was smoke
Spiring its tall black cenotaph to the sky;
And we stood on our decks saying: Alas, alas,
That great city Babylon, that mighty city,
For in one hour is thy judgment come.

Belshazzar

That day in the city there were banners slung
Across the streets, from balconies and chimneys,
Swinging in the wind like smoke, and telegraph poles
Were hung with geraniums; military bands
Marched down the thoroughfares and bugles rang
Against the plate-glass frontages. And in that night
There were fireworks in the public parks at twilight,
Laburnums of flame that flowered and fell through the air,
And high on the hill the palace windows blazed
Like the shell of a house on fire. And in that night
The uniforms moved along the lobbies, gold and scarlet,
Gold and blue, and shoulders were sugared with jewels
Under the hanging icicles of chandeliers.
They poured the yellow wine in the grey silver,
The red in the yellow gold, and plates were piled
With quails and nightingales and passion fruit,
And the air was a fume of music. And in that night
The King sat above his court, speaking to none,
Small and grotesque there in a high-backed chair,
His hands gripping the carved griffins, his eyes
Like halves of hard-boiled eggs. He stared at the wall,
At the bare plaster above the footmen's heads.
The music and laughter ceased, the people were silent,
They put down their forks and raised no cup to the mouth,
But turned and stared at the wall where the King was staring.
And there was nothing on the wall at all.

The Raven

The raven flew above the screes, above the rocks,
Where the bare bones of the mountain broke through the skin,
And rain trickled to the black tarn, and lichen
Grew like gangrene on the splintered knuckles.
The raven flew down the long wedge of the dale,
Above the upland dykes and slate and cobble walls
Piled against the high waves of the fells.
With slower corrugations of its wings
It dropped below the bracken cut for bedding
To where green oats were sown on the brant fell,
And the lyle herdwicks fed in the wet pastures
For the grass was thicker there and orchids and burnet grew.
The raven suddenly stepped steeply up the air
Seeing a man sitting beside the beck,
An old man with a beard white as may. The green
Water wound like bindweed round the rocks,
And burst into buds and elderflowers of foam;
Rowans and hawthorns creamed and bubbled with blossom
And splashed their petals on the old man's head,
Who felt them not at all nor the thin white rain.
The raven soared on a lifting wind
And flew to the farm beyond the mosses,
Dropped like a hawk to the stackyard, scared
The fowls with a thick black beak, and snatched the bread
Which the farmer's wife had scattered. It flew to the dale
And dropped the bread to the man, who dipped it in the water,
And ate it like a sop. The raven flew away
Knowing no reason nor questioning, knowing neither

The man's face nor his name, for there was never a place
For names in the brain of a raven, 'though its eyes
Were a dove's eyes in a black corvine head.

The Wood of the Self-Murdered

The trees against the mountain's groin
Pitch wigwams in a zigzag line.
Pelts of pine and spruce and fir
Are tented in the cloudy air;
The western light slides down the wide
Slant of the branches of brown hide.

No creature tracks the furry dark,
Not owl nor weasel is awake;
The wind grunts by and rubs its flanks
And hears the groans of rocking trunks,
And the dead drip of the red rain
As the mist blankets down again.

On every twig and branch are risen
Blobs of blood like dark red resin
That drizzle to the ground and stain
Grass and brambleleaf and thorn;
The bark is blistered and the wood
Crusted with scabs and boils of blood.

These are the wooden souls of men
Who broke the life in their own bone;
With rope round neck or knife in throat
They turned their backs upon the light,
And now their fears creak in the breeze,
In blood-red darkness, turned to trees.

Beneath the soil the long shoots bore
To limestone and to iron ore,
Where through the rock the waters ooze
Red as the sap in the live trees,
And becks swill seaward, rich as wine,
The haemorrhage of the split mine.

Empires and towns are buried here
That stabbed themselves or died of fear.
Towers and terraces crack and fall,
And sink into the sandy soil,
And, bleeding like a running sore,
Do penance in the broken ore.

The First Day of Autumn

For Kathleen Raine

Now steady on the wind the white gull lies,
And the wind wavering from west to east:
To th' equinoctial sun man lifts his eyes.
Midway between an angel and a beast.

The mountains push their spiky steeples high;
The sum of creatures adds to less than one
In the bright hierarchy of earth and sky –
Angel and man and beast and flower and stone.

Michaelmas

Like a hound with nose to the trail
The 'bus follows the road;
The road leaps up the hill.
In the valley the railway line is carved like a groove in wood;
The little towns smoke in the hollows;
The slagbanks are grey beneath the brown, bludgeoning fell.

This is the day the air has eyes,
And the Devil falls like hail
From the bright and thundering skies,
And soaks into soil and rock,
And the bad blood rises in nettle and dock,
And toadstools burst like boils between the toes of the trees.

The war that began in heaven still goes on.
Thorn trees twist like spears,
The owl haunts the grain,
The coursed rabbit weeps icicles of tears;
But the feathers of the clouds foretell
St Michael's victory in the purged and praising rain.

Shortest Day, 1942

For N. W.

The damp December light
Settles like fog on roofs
And gable-ends of slate;
The wind blows holes in the sky; the rain
Shines on the road like tin,
And rain-drops hang on the privet, round and white.

Behind a freestone wall,
Between the houses and the street,
In twelve or less square feet
Of tarmac and black soil
Blooms the purple primula
Bright as a lollipop or an aniseed ball.

And so a smile will flower,
A kiss like a child's laugh, or more
Like a friendly terrier's bark,
While the town huddles beneath a dark
Drizzle of misery, and the wind
Flings down sleet from the frozen fells of war.

Now in the Time of this Mortal Life

Frost is tight upon the land
Constricts it with a bony hand,
Yet with blade sharp as a nail
The immanent crocus drills the soil.
Man's nerves aver his spinal wish
And feel the Word becoming Flesh.

God watches soil and spirit mated,
And consecrates what he created,
By raising manhood unto God,
By raising raisins unto blood;
The sacramental prongs reach down
And lift earth to the skies again.
Incarnate God shines brighter than
Flower or frost, or sea or sun.
The Spirit in the limbs of man
Hardens like a skeleton,
And the earth feels a new life burrow
Along its stony bones like marrow.
For now the ritual seed is sown
To grow the stalk to bear the grain
To yield the flour to make the bread
That sinful hands shall turn to God.

The hooks of love are in our limbs
And hoist through the scholastic times
When bursting bud and bomb deny
The Manichaean heresy.
And man finds voice to curse once more

The evil in the holy fear,
And man finds heart to praise again
The hope within the evil pain,
Christ-knife heals the wound it prunes,
And carves its gospel on the bones,
That man may hear what God has heard,
And feel the Flesh becoming Word.

Carol

Mary laid her Child among
  The bracken-fronds of night –
And by the glimmer round His head
  All the barn was lit.

Mary held her Child above
  The miry, frozen farm –
And by the fire within His limbs
  The resting roots were warm.

Mary hid her Child between
  Hillocks of hard sand –
By singing water in His veins
  Grass sprang from the ground.

Mary nursed her Child beside
  The gardens of a grave –
And by the death within His bones
  The dead became alive.

Shepherds' Carol

When the frost was white on the wool of our flocks
And stars like hailstones fell on the rocks,
When we held our fingers tight to the dirk
And sharpened our eyes on the slaty dark
That blocked the ghyll and blackened the scree,
It was never a light we thought to see.

When the light blazed on the spikes of the fell
We remembered the burning barns in the dale;
When our collies pricked up their ears, and we
Harked to the warning wind from the sea
That creaked in the reeds by the frozen mere,
It never was music we thought to hear.

When the music clamoured across the tarns
And voices rang from the singing cairns
Of a holy chieftain, a warrior priest,
Blown from the wondering isles of the west
On a full tide and a pulling wind,
It was never a child we thought to find.

But the music we heard and the light we saw
And the child we found in a cot of straw.
When we took the lambs that were dropped in the snow
And ran to the stones by the sacred tree,
It was never ourselves we thought to give –
But we gave ourselves that the lambs might live.

For the New Year

The stars wheel past the windows
Like flocks of winter sparrows;
The bell clangs out the hours,
And frost sparkles like stars,
And the wind blows up the dawn
With spring behind it and rain
And the spikes of daffodils
And June on fire in the hills.
The apples crowd the bough
Beneath the frosty Plough,
And autumn snow is blown
White as a harvest moon
On currant and raspberry cane.
And the wild ganders fly
Nightly across the sky.
The seasons flit like linnets,
And years whirl past like planets,
And the earth's orbit mars
The changeless map of stars.
The splintered light which now
Gently probes my eye
Is of a star that burned
When the Scots fired the land,
When the Norsemen robbed the dales
And hacked their names on the fells,
Or when the iceberg lakes
Elbowed among the rocks
And carried the Devil's stone

To the hill above the town,
Where through my dormer bay
Drizzles the Milky Way.

Poem for Epiphany

Three Kings stepped out of my body,
Walked across the sand by the wild sea
From December into January.

A King stepped out of my head,
And before him the sand was red
And the sea gold,
And he beheld
The landscape like an empire and found in
Even a sycamore leaf the plan of his domain.
And he offered the gold of his sight
The regimen of his thought
To the Child born that night.

A King stepped out of my breast
Who had the bearing of a priest.
To him the moon's movement
Was a sacrament,
And the taste of water and of wine,
The touch of bread and the weight of a stone.
And he offered the frankincense of the heart,
Prayer swung in the censer on the charcoal alight,
To the Child born that night.

A King stepped out of my loins,
And black as grapes were his skin and his veins.
In him was the anger of sex
Where the blood like a sea on the shingle breaks,
The pride of living, the longing for further birth

Because of the presentiment of death.
And he offered the myrrh of tiredness, the untight'ning of the
  fingers from the nerve's root
To the Child born that night.

Three Kings stepped out of my body
But only my two eyes between the three –
Only my two eyes and the wild skies to see.

The Ride to Jerusalem

And he answered and said unto them, I tell you that, if these
should hold their peace, the stones would immediately cry out.
(Luke xix, 40)

The colt is tethered to the appointed gate
The password known: 'The Lord hath need of him';
The trees are ready – this year Easter's late –
And willows wave their feather-fronds of palm.

The starlings practise on the chimney pots;
The thoroughfares of time are open wide;
Soon, now, the eyes shall weep for the blind streets,
The healing voice shall speak to the deaf road.

The window-sills are empty; no crowds wait;
Here at the pavement's edge I watch alone.
Master, like sunlight strike my slaty heart
And ask not acclamations from the stone.

Gethsemane

Among these evergreens the bitter spring
   Spreads on my head like stonecrop on grey stone,
Yellow to eyes and pepper to the tongue,
   But never known to the impervious bone.

Catkins remind me only how the year
   Brought that day hope, and disappointment, this.
How shall I witness what is happening where
   The dark green branches prophesy a kiss?

My courage sleeps like boulders where a bird
   May perch, or yellow surf of stonecrop break.
For this I cannot ask forgiveness, Lord –
   Forgive me that the trees remained awake.

Song for Pelagius

When the rain rains upward,
  And the rivers siphon the sea,
When the becks run backward,
  And the sunset swells into day,
When the seed cracks into flower,
  And the flower folds into bud,
    Man of a rib
  Shall work a wife for God.

When oaks and elders
  Pump sap into the soil,
When props and pitshafts
  Stuff the earth with coal,
When the bright equator
  Illuminates the sun,
    Man of his will
  Shall hoist himself to heaven.

The Preachers

The Lord God smiled
  At the mild words
As He heard St Francis
  Preach to the birds.

Preach of a tree
  With berries on,
That a woman ate
  And gave to a man;

The juice was sweet
  But tart the core,
No herb in field
  Their gripes could cure;

But another tree
  Grew redder fruit,
And there God grafted
  The antidote.

Sparrow and starling,
  Jackdaw and rook
Perched on slates
  And chimney stack.

Tits trapezed
  Upon the spouts,
Starlings dropped lime
  Like marguerites.

They sang to the saint
  With scornful beak:
'The berries give *us*
  No bellyache.

'But the pips split
  And sprout in man,
And through the thighs
  The roots grow down.'

The Lord God laughed
  At the wild fancies
As He heard the birds
  Preach to St Francis.

The Council of the Seven Deadly Sins

Across the shingle to the land
The winds from the sea blow the sand
And little dunes like mole-hills rear
Day by day in the town square.
The council men with spade and shovel
Try to make the roadway level,
But the winds whirl and the bents bind
And the rain cakes the stalking sand.
Gutters are blocked with yellow weed,
The sand is puddled into mud;
Restharrow, stonecrop and sweet gale
Clog the ruts of lorry wheel;
Nettles prick up dusty lugs,
And thistles thrust through broken flags,
And where the rusty ragworts grow
The slow sand drifts like dry brown snow.
It blows through window and through door,
Along the lobby, up the stair,
Drops like sugar in the tea,
Like pepper in the cooking stew,
Till every child of the town owns
Sand in his blood, sand in his bones.

Inside the school where sea winds rumble
The parish councillors assemble.
The Chairman at the teacher's table
Rubs his jaw like a smooth cobble.
His chin is granite, eyes are flint
That on his trusted colleagues glint.

Here sits the oldest councillor;
His cheeks are red as iron ore,
Around his teeth the plump lips roll
Bent in an avaricious smile.
He is the one who always knows
Where a building contract goes,
And where the County Council grants
Will give a chance to raise the rents.
He'd melt the sand if it would yield
Half a pennyweight of gold;
He'd boil the sea if it would leave
Silver in the weedy sieve;
He'd hack the living limbs of earth
If bony rocks had any worth,
And wring the guts of the red ore
If they would give one blood-drop more.

The second councillor is there,
Sitting upright in his chair.
His face is lean and whippet-jawed
And blue as slate with three-day beard:
His eyes from out their sockets bore
Like corkscrews at the stubborn air;
His lips, like whetstones in his cheeks
Sharpen the words that his tongue speaks.
He will hate his worthy hire
If someone gets a penny more;
He will scorn the job he does
If someone works a minute less.
He bites the smile off his own face
Envious of other's happiness,
And shuts his eyes on heaven's blue
Because it blesses bishops too.

The farmer's member from the dale
Always returned without a poll,
Slovenly sprawls in his squat seat,
Third of this company of state.
His slothful eyes are dull as smoke,
His tribly pushed back to his neck,
His ribs are flabby and his stomach
Hangs from his waist like a full hammock.
He gives no thought of future peril
If earth's rich womb be laboured sterile,
Nor cares the price of a dead wick
What happens to the men he'll sack.
Content the country's sound in limb
So long as nothing troubles him.

The fourth good governor has eyes
Purple with blood and dull with booze,
Red as ripe strawberries, his lip
Slobbers with juice like dripping tap.
Down his throat he'd quickly swill
The bitter sea if it were ale,
And, gluttonous as fire, he'd eat
The sand if it were sausage meat,
And stuff Scawfell inside his belly
If it were lamb and currant jelly.

Bright as a rose-hip in September
Lolls the only woman member;
Light and lecherous, her eye
Signals the Chairman jauntily –
A heavy scent, like foetid flower
Rotting in the hothouse air,
Puffs from her curls, crinkled as crêpe,

When she shakes her lacquered nape.
For hers is love that bears no fruit,
Barren at its acid root;
Hers is the slang of lechery,
The mean excursions of the eye,
Cheapjack commerce of breast and thigh
On sandhill or in passage-way.
The quickened sap of budding seed
Will never flow along her blood;
Marriage and motherhood she'll miss
For sake of one more drunken kiss.

The sixth man stalks about the room,
His read hair angry as a flame,
His eyes like white-hot poker-ends,
Swollen his veins like gouty hands.
He'll fight the Council for his plan
To throttle Hitler, bomb Berlin,
Teach foreigners some English fashions,
By cleaning up the French and Russians,
And turn around again and show
A lesson to the USA
It's heaven to him in any weathers
If he can make a hell for others,
Satisfied only when all action
Explodes in wild dissatisfaction.

Silent as slate the Chairman sits,
Waiting till the talk abates,
Proud his eyes as polished ore,
His mouth incised with a stiff sneer.
Knowing he need do nought to check it
Because the Council's in his pocket.

And any vote that he may cast
Will be unanimously passed.

The sand against the window-sill
Blows like a drizzle of fine hail;
Beyond the sea, like a mad dog,
The wind worries the vermin fog.

The Garden of the Innocent

I

In the evening, the cool time, between sunset and moonrise,
Under a star un-named of a pagan name,
Under the green sky, under the broad leaves,
Under the dark green shadows of the brown trees,
On the darker grass and moss and ground-ivy
That scents the heels which crush it and the dusk,
Among the dew and the wood-sorrel, in the cool of the day,
Move the creatures who have never been me.

The light on their limbs is pale as a hazel kernel,
Smooth as peeled bark as they walk between the pines,
Where the dark cones open in the dry air,
Where the squirrels are friendly, the voles without fear,
And the throstles call from the resinous branches.
There as the green light ebbs from the sky
They sleep below the anonymous constellations,
Undisturbed by chatter of sedge-birds from the river.

These are the creatures who have never been me.
Slayers of dragons have been me, and tamers of snakes,
And those who pressed the fangs in their own flesh,
And those who lied for fear of snakes or killed for lust of them,
Those have all been me; but never these,
Who heard the voice in the upper branches and were unafraid.
I also have heard the voice in the upper branches,
And my heart tripped over itself, my feet hesitated,
My tongue was unable to speak and my ears to be deaf.
And all who have been me have heard and feared;

[84]

Even the conqueror of dragons, even the sinner
Who bursts from the root of his sin like a tree on fire.
But not these,
These who have never been me.

II

Where is that garden? Who will find it?
And who explore the land around it?
Who interrogate the wall,
And who confront the fiery stile?
I leave the clearing in my brain,
Where the eyes let in the sun,
And search the skull-shaped forest there,
Where scurfy leaves grow thick as hair.
Between the pine trunks, red as blood,
Like a long wound is gashed the road.
Straight and deep it stretches forth
In front, behind, or south and north,
Backward and forward is the same,
Whither I go or whence I came.
The moss corrodes the bark of fir,
The ivy hugs it like a bear;
The dormered larches' tiles of snow,
Opaque as pot, make dusk of day;
Agarics' phosphorescent light
On rotting leaves makes dusk of night.
No spring disturbs the hemlock seeds;
The bittercress creaks barren pods,
That tell on withered calendar
No hour of day, no month of year.
The beck is frozen to the rock,
And time is still as a dead clock.

[85]

The darkness skulks in crevices;
A rabbit squeals at a stoat's eyes.
Where the spruce bends like a green claw
The furry silence slinks away.
The fir trees scream like knife on bone,
The sap like blood pounds through the pine.
I fear the voice will crack the sky
And slash the neutralizing snow,
For there's no garden in these trees –
And if there were there'd be the voice.
The blood of pines congeals like rind
To hide what I set out to find;
I pray foreover to be lost
Blown through the mist as a deaf ghost,
And call on death or forest fire
To thwart my eyes of my desire.

III

February is the month when the year stretches itself.
The buds which have rested since autumn in their gummy
   cocoons
Stir like a butterfly waking from hibernation;
The willows cock up silver furry ears;
The rooks clear their throats and springclean their nests in the
   elms;
        The hedgesparrows begin to sing
        Like a kettle simmering.

The ducks quadrille in the farmyard and drink at the pond,
Holding their necks up high to let the water run down.
They dig their bills into the mud and know no gluttony;
A cur sniffs after a bitch and knows no lechery;

A weasel bites into a pullet and knows no cruelty;
A pig lies in the straw and knows no sloth;
>A stallion polishes its hide
>And knows no pride.

These cannot tell me – nor the jay in the woods,
Nor the wolf in the forest, nor the python in the jungle,
Nor the beasts who fleshed the bones we find in the hills.
The dinotherium, the mammoth, the sabre-toothed tiger,
Nor the creature with the ape-like skull who learned to look at
    fire;
>These cannot show
>The way I should go.

For these there are no bounds to the garden, neither inside nor
    outside,
These who do not hear the voice, and, without hearing, obey.
They do not choose whether to know or know not,
Neither choose rightly nor choose wrongly.
They do not know what it is to choose or choose not.
They know neither temptation nor conscience, choose neither
    innocence nor sin.
>For them the thistle is food,
>And the nettle a bed.
>For them there is no fence of fire,
>No past to long for,
>No future to fear.

IV

The river that waters the garden
  Drains all lands under the skies –
From the four angles of the square earth
  It draws its four tributaries.

The first stream gushes in a land of gold,
  The second from the brown sand flows,
The third from a valley of green olive trees,
  The fourth from the blue snows.

I followed the course of the fourth stream
  And climbed above the plains
To gaze down into the garden
  From the high mountains.

I sought the source of the fourth stream
  Through moss and rocky gully,
Where the white mist fumes above the blue snows
  Like foam on a blue sea.

I took no heed of the warnings
  In the village beside the glacier,
For I longed to see the landscape below me
  Through the cold air.

But the snow was smudged on the hump of the fell
  Was it mist or the shoulder
Of bear or mountain-ape or man?
  Or the shadow of a boulder?

I remembered the legends of the upland village
   Of the fear in the beds of the married,
Of the children whose footsteps were rubbed out like chalk,
   Of the women who miscarried.

But I told myself that no man nor beast
   Could follow me there;
No warm-blooded being from the plains
   Could live in that frozen air.

The toothed wind snarled through the larches
   And crunched the brittle hail,
And I heard a howl answering the wind's howl
   Like a dog growling at the gale.

The mist twisted in the hairy pines
   And looped the ermine snow;
The shadows were solid and furred and grey –
   As I moved through the trees I saw them follow.

The stoats of snow were at my throat,
   The spruces clawed at my hair,
But I feared only that the snowman
   Might bring his human malice there.

I drew the geometric triple pikes
   In the sexless snow,
But like blots of ink I found the tracks
   Of a man's heel and toe.

No cloven hoof, no buzzard's talons,
   But a naked human toe –
I reeled, and slid down the frozen slope
   To the valley below.

In the village the women nurse me,
   With warm hands and warm breath;
But I fear when they thaw my limbs into life
   My soul will freeze into death.

v

The circle undrawn is never the circle drawn;
The flower in the seed is never the flower in the bud;
The child in the mind is never the child in the womb.

The picture on the canvas betrays the vision in the brain;
The lust in the loins betrays the love in the heart;
The ape on the mountain betrays the man in the garden.

The garden is not to be longed for or regretted;
The birds are not to be understood or ignored;
The creatures are not to be imitated or envied;

There is grass on the earth though the nettles grow through our
   ankles;
There is fruit on the trees though the brambles tear at our
   thighs;
There is manhood in our fingers though the ape howls through
   our blood.

That to which we cannot return is not to be found before us:
There is no other garden beyond the bright sea.
The nettle will follow the opportune harrow,
The thorn increase in the blandishments of spring.
Not in the prospectus of a blind tomorrow,
But in the scything of nettles shall we find bread.
In the burning of thorns shall we find warmth.
The hand that is stung by nettles shall know deftness,
The foot that is pricked by thorns shall develop strength.

In the garden, in the morning, in the experimental light,
Hearing the birdsong, and the still-unthroated voice,
Move the creatures whom I can never be.

The Holy Mountain

Dawn flares like a bonfire behind the eastern fell,
Rockets up to the sky and burns out the stars,
Licks up the mists as an oven licks up steam,
Pours down the rocks and the screes like molten slag,
Gushes down the water-courses, down forces and ghylls,
Spreads like oil on the tarns, like burning bracken on the tops,
Till the peaks blaze like braziers.
And lower on the slopes the larches catch the flame,
Bristling with fire they crackle beneath the brass rocks,
In the metallic forest, by the steel rods of birches,
And the fire burns white as a furnace.
The dale, split out of the base of the fell,
Is brimful of light and open to the day,
And the river roots among the shingle and stirs the silt
Yellow as gold-dust in the cracks of the rocks.

In the bend of the river, beneath the crags and the rowans,
The garden is here and the garden was always here.
The soil is brown and fertile, ground from the rocks by the
    rains,
Carried down by the river and terraced at the turn.
The orchard grows on the slope that slants to the sun –
Damson, bullace and crab, and gean, the wild cherry,
White as lambs in spring. And the flowers of the dale,
Bigger than those of the fells, frailer than those of the fields:
The globe-flower, like a lemon, quartered but unpeeled;
The bell-flower, hanging its blue chime from a steeple of nettle-
    leaves,

Betony and cow-wheat, golden-rod and touch-me-not,
And in the woods, enchanter's nightshade,
And by the river, daffodils.

The wind idles among the alders and moves the branches,
And tinkles the catkins of the hazels, blowing pollen from tree
  to tree;
The cresses flick their pods to the rocks above;
The coltsfoot lets slip its down like floating spiders;
And daffodil bulbs set sail to the lower meadows,
But only to evangelize beyond the boundary of the garden,
For there is no need of seeding, here, where there is no dying.
Yet the primrose relinquishes its petals and the willows their
  leaves
For a time of rest, of waiting, of re-creation.
And that there be no corruption in the garden,
The fungi flicker up and burn the fallen leaves,
Purple, red and yellow, sulphur-tuft and fly-agaric,
They glow like coke through the nights of the darker season.
The clouds blow in from the sea and burst on the fell.
The rain falls, the beck fills, the water disintegrates the stone,
And the soil is sifted down for the fulfilment of the garden.

II

A Jew upon Mount Ararat
Beside the cairn-like altar sat,
Saw in the rocks above the lake
The murals of the Pentateuch;
Saw Adam, bigger than the hills,
Name the invented animals,
Saw him watch the angels crowd
The Jacob's ladders of the cloud;

[93]

Saw him hang rubies round his thighs,
Clustered thick as blackberries,
Hoist on his shoulders golden gear
And, barefoot, walk through stones of fire –
A second angel, from his birth
Appointed viceroy of the earth.

And unto Adam sons were born,
And sons unto his sons in turn,
Till the wild lands were populous
With men and women of his race.
The girls walked in the river meadows;
Their hair fell down their cheeks like shadows,
Brown as raisins, soft as rain,
Smudging the whiteness of their skin.
Soon they throw away their clothes
And each one like a linnet bathes
Her body in the singing ripples.
Their shoulders were as round as apples,
Their arms were smooth as grass, their bosoms
White as sunlight on the blossoms,
And they were safe from all men's glances
Behind the pear and damson fences.
But from the angels in the sky
No trees could shutter them away.
The Watchers, who from heaven's wall
Mission to Jehovah's will,
Bored with adoring, hugged their pride
And planned themselves to be adored.
They longed to leave desires burned
In the girls' flesh like a red brand,
To see the God-shaped human limbs
Rheumatic with an angel's crimes.

They leaped the shining bannister
And parachuted through the air,
Descending thick and white and slow
As Noah's downpour turned to snow.
Each angel chose a girl for mate,
But scarcely could they consummate
The clash of spirit and of flesh
(Like mist raped by the lightning's flash)
When, from the cloud's high gable-ends,
Archangels fell on the four winds.
They snatched the Watchers from their lovers
And whirled them down by the four rivers,
There to freeze till Judgment enter
The caves of ice at the earth's centre.
Still held, by love, at fever heat,
The girls' blood in their bodies wrought
The angels' semen into bones,
And gave it heart and flesh and brains.
They bore their babies at full moon
With prayer and sacrifice and pain,
Laid them on beds of pigeons' feathers
And mourned the wings of the lost fathers.
The children spat as mothers kissed,
Fought in their arms, refused the breast,
And, agile as a new-hatched adder,
Ran off and searched for a cow's udder.
Within a week they grew to boys
Who ripped the branches from the trees;
Within a month they grew to men
Who butchered bulls on the wild plain.
Within a year they grew to giants
Who set fire to the corn like truants,
And tossed the rocks about, and tore

The antlers off the living deer,
Bred and brought forth among the screes
Mesozoic prodigies.
Creatures with necks as long as larches,
With legs like oaks and tails like birches:
Creatures from shoulder-blade to knee
Upholstered like a plush settee,
Or jointed along spine and hip,
And plated like a battle-ship.
They hunted horses on the hawes.
And broke the backbones of the cows,
Till, as they grew old, their skin
Like rusty armour weighed them down.
And they left chase of pads and hooves,
And dragged themselves to die in caves.
But before they died they taught
Their cruelty to fox and stoat;
Taught the raven how to rip
The eyes and skull of dying sheep;
Taught surgery of claw and beak
To owl and kestrel, kite and hawk;
Taught the pike to open jaws
Wide enough to bolt a dace;
Taught the adder to exchange
Reptile teeth for small syringe.
And in their rotting carcases
Bred blow-flies, mites, mosquitoes, fleas,
And pain and death moved through the dales
With claws and fangs, with wings and tails.
But no live thing of earth or hell
Walks on the boulders of the fell.

A Jew upon Mount Ararat
Prophesied of evil heart,
Of angel's blood in human veins,
Death and the necessary sins,
Till the mists rose on Easter night
And darkness blotted him from sight.

III

Higher than the skies are the fires of heaven,
    Deeper than the rocks the frost of hell,
And the garden is here that was always here,
    Here, beneath the fell.

And in the garden there is an orchard,
    And in the orchard there is a tree,
And on the tree there was an apple,
    The rarest the sun could see.

Green as the rain the apple grew,
    Green as the clouds blown westerly,
Green as the mist on salt marshes,
    Green as the sea.

The sun stared at its southerly cheek,
    As red as the sun the apple grew,
And the redder juice beneath the skin
    Shone like sunlight through.

The trees their liturgical banners waved
    Throughout the ferials of the year;
Blossoms were stitched in silk, and leaves
    Embroidered there.

Green as the rain, red as the sun,
   Still the apple bigger grew,
Air and fire it drew through leaves,
   Water and earth through roots it drew.

'The rock is deep but hell is deeper,
   The sky is high but heaven is higher,
And between them hang I,'the apple sang,
   'Earth, air, water, fire.'

The blossoms shrivelled on that tree,
   The fruit was as small as a hip or a sloe,
But the one apple grew till the bough bent
   As beneath snow.

And the apple sang to the bright air:
   'Thus does heaven its favourites bless,
For the elements are transmuted to
   My apple-ness.'

Red as the sun the ripe skin shone,
   The core and pulp began to swell,
Till the short stalk snapped beneath the weight
   And the apple fell.

The apple rotted on the ground,
   Rotted in the grass by the roots of trees.
And through the soil the proud rot ran
   Like a disease.

Grass wrapped its roots round the roots of grass
    And sulked into a parasite.
Ivy sucked the oak's green blood
    And dragged itself towards the light.

The mistletoe broke from its slender trunk
    Which once the leaves and seedlets bore,
And left its berries like orphaned babies
    At the crab-apple's door.

Fungi moved from fallen leaves
    And ate into the living wood,
Spread up the bark and along the boughs.
    Laid cancer on the bud.

Dry rot gouged out the heart of the elm,
    The sycamore leaf was black with blight,
The yellow corn was brown with rust,
    The green with mildew white.

Smaller, more cunning, the fungi grew
    In the living leaf and flower and bud;
Till shrunk to bacilli they multiplied
    In the living blood.

The septic blossoms dropped like scabs,
    The rotting leaves fell from the tree,
And the heat of the summer in the festering grass
    Bred cruelty.

The purple butterwort held its flower
   Like a child's mask above an evil smile;
The sundew set its five green traps
   With quiet guile.

Now seeding can scarcely keep pace with dying,
   As flowers bloom and fruit and fall,
And the need for seed rises like fever
   In them all.

There is no time, now, to colonize
   Beyond the garden, by beck or well,
And the wind blows back the scattered pods
   From the bare fell.

IV

For we know that together the whole creation cries,
Leaves find tongues like wolves and howl to the skies,
      And beasts howl to the moon.
The earth groans in the travail of birth;
All things that live have knowledge of death,
      All things that move of pain.
There is no rest, no refuge, there is no predicted hope.
      On the high down,
The rabbit, caught by the foot, to escape the trap
      Gnaws through the bone.

The vine grows on the terraces under the sun;
Its roots tap the soil, its leaves catch the air and the rain,
      And the grapes hang there.
In the crook of the dale, below the rocks and the fern,

The wind blows from seaward and bends the corn,
        And the fields are white as flour.
Rain, rock, broken to wine and bread,
        Are formed now into the Blessed Body.
The baptismal river floods to the will of God,
        And tallow burns to His glory.

The earth shall be crushed like an olive for the sacred oil,
Fermented like the grape, ground like corn in the mill,
        And burned like lard.
The earth shall burn to the sky; like the six
Candles before the altar shall burn the six peaks
        To the glory of the Lord:
Everest, Sinai, and the seven-fold hill of Rome,
        The tripod of creeds,
Helvellyn, megalithic Gable, and Wetherlam,
        Burning above the orchards.

The fell shall rise white above the six-pronged blaze
Like steel in a furnace, high as the skies,
        Deep as the ice of hell.
And the creatures shall come from the orchard, the dale, and
    the shore,
Shall gaze at the blaze and pass through the fire
        And walk on the fell.
The wolf and the sheep together, the young wolf and the lamb,
        The fox and the chicken,
The weasel and the rabbit through the fire shall come
        And lie down in the bracken.

The kestrel, there, shall eat haws like the throstle,
The owl, like the goldfinch shall feed on the thistle,
        The stoat shall eat grass like the hare.

In the becks the pike shall play with the trout,
The stickleback shall swim beneath the heron's feet.
Nothing shall be hurtful there.
In that holy mountain like the sun the Word
Shall shine on rock and beast and tree,
For the earth shall be full of the knowledge of the Lord
As the waters cover the sea.

Part II – See Genesis VI. verses 1?4.
Also Ezekiel XXVIII. verses 13?15.
Part IV – See Romans VIII. verses 18?22
and Isaiah XI. verses 6?9.

The Bow in the Cloud

I

White and thin, the paper moon rides high
Among the yellow clouds, dead and dry as an oyster-shell,
With chippings of shadow and a lobsided curve.
It rears above the fells, following the forgotten dawn
Along the moors that stretch to the estuary
And steers to the western sky. There as the sun bears down
The orange light drains over the rim of the sea,
And the tide holds back from the flat wet sands
That darken from tawny to brown, where little pools
Are stranded like starfish in the rippling ribs.

The salt lies pale at the dead edge of the sea
Among the broken mussels and the rotting bladderwrack,
The cracked pots and corks and driftwood dry as tinder,
Where the blackbacked gull barks above the shingle,
And the stubble beard of marram on the jowl of the dune
Bristles beside the sea-holly's dry grey hair. Only the sand
Shifts and slithers beneath the fingerings of the wind.

The wooden groins run back from the shore
To the long seawall that hoards in its rocky cordon
The pitshafts with wheels like a sailor's helm,
The rubble red and dark in the sandy dusk,
The mines where once the purple ore was broken
To boom as a gun or ring out as a clattering peal.

In the cobbled chapel on the dunes
With its tower held like a bell-buoy above the angled wave of
    the roof,
No clapper knocks for evensong nor even to knell the hearse,
But the iron silts with sand beneath the yellowing moon.
It waits for the time when the bell again will swing
And the iron crack in the wind and the boulders ring like steel
And the moon and the pebbles and the dead sand on the shore
Fall into file at the eighth word of creation,
And the dumb sea shout with the voice that once was shamed
    by man.

II

    Old Tyson was a farmer,
        A statesman of the fell;
    He put his stock on the Plymouth Rock
        And preached of the devil and hell.

    When the sun went down on Sundays,
        And the throstles sang in the trees,
    He tilted his beard to the green sky
        And bared his hair to the breeze.

    He prayed to the Lord for rain,
        From whence all blessing flows,
    And stretched his fingers across the beck
        To see if the water rose.

    As he stretched his fingers across the beck
        To see if the water were higher,
    A stickleback leapt into his hands
        Like a spark from a cracking fire.

Its spiny hump in the sunshine
    Was red as a rooster's comb;
Its tail was green as gooseberries
    With clots of hairy foam.

It turned its eyes on Tyson,
    Its tiny voice spoke clear:
'Do not throw me back in the busy beck,
    Tyson, keep me here.

'There in the world of water
    Fish on each other prey;
I'm so small I shall soon be devoured;
    Tyson, take me away.'

Old Tyson took the stickleback
    And put it in a bowl;
And it grew till it burst its china shell
    And swallowed the pieces whole.

He put it next in a barrel,
    Then in a brown lake,
But it grew till it heaved like an island
    And dammed the flooding beck.

Old Tyson took the stickleback
    And put it in a wagon,
And carted it down to the wild shore
    Where the sea roared like a dragon.

The waves were bright and fiery
  And crackled as they broke;
And the wind shook the sparks of foam
  And blew away the smoke.

Old Tyson tossed the stickleback
  Into the burning sea,
And the great fish wallowed in waves of flame
  And grew exceedingly.

It grew till it filled the ocean
  And swallowed the smoking tide,
And from its snout a horn grew out
  Tall as a mariner's guide.

'Oh, listen, Tyson, listen,
  And watch the wide moon round,
For when I spew the ocean up
  The whole world will be drowned.

'Go home and build a vessel
  Of the pines upon the fell,
And watch for the breaking of the moon,
  For the cracking of the bell.

'Take in all birds and animals,
  Two of every kind;
Take seed of grass and herb and weed,
  And watch for the green wind.

'And when the waters burn the sand,
  And hot waves melt the mud,
Tie your boat to my tall horn,
  And fly before the flood.'

Old Tyson took a hatchet
  Chopped down mountain trees,
And built a ship like a floating barn
  To ride the fiery seas.

He gathered seeds of barley,
  Wheat and oats and rye,
Dog-grass and dock and pimpernel,
  Chickweed and chicory,

The feathery seeds of thistles,
  The long black pods of broom,
The spores of bracken and lady-fern –
  For each one he found room.

He brought the horse from the stable,
  He brought the cow from the byre,
He drove them into the barn-like ship
  Beside the lapping fire.

The animals came from the fellside,
  Fox and hare and rat,
hedgehog and weasel, rabbit and vole,
  Side by side they sat.

The birds flew in from the marshes,
　　Buzzard and bunting together
And not a claw hooked at an eye
　　Nor a beak stabbed at a feather.

The great fish rolled in the ocean
　　And belched out flaming spray;
The mountains rocked like a sinking ship,
　　And the moon was yellow as hay.

Old Tyson counted the wide moon round:
　　The clouds were green and strange.
He raised his eyes to the western skies
　　And watched for the wind to change.

III

Nearer and nearer the brass moon swings
Down through the green sky in narrowing rings.
Faster and faster it cruises round the earth,
Swelling from emptiness to greatest girth
In twenty days or less, and each moon wider
Than those that went before in the follow-my-leader,
Till the yellow globe in its tightening grooves
Blots out constellations as it moves.
The sea heaves after it, like restless crowds,
Elbows through groin and breakwater, spreads
Over the low-lying marshes, shoulders into the shore,
And each spring tide digs deeper in the dune's soft core.
And now the moon's enormous crust
Crumbles like dried mud into dust,
And the sky is darkened with a wide stain
Of coughing clouds of dry and choking rain,

And the moon shudders as if in pain,
And its jaundiced skin rots at the pores
And breaks out into boils and sores,
Which drop away like scabs, ignite, and fall
On the cringing continents as fiery hail,
And the joints of the mountains crack
As the earth arches its rocky back.
The sea bludgeons the shore's long flanks,
Bursts through the dykes like a fleet of tanks,
Smashes like a heel on a matchbox the roofs of the town,
Breaks chimneystack and derrick down,
Tears belfry from steeple, tombstone from grave,
While the broken bell cracks upon the wave.
The water floods the lowlands and the dales,
And fills the ghylls and gullies of the fells,
Till Tyson, leaning from his vessel, sees
Flooks flap in the tops of the trees,
And jellyish flung on the slant of the screes.
Terns loop above the parsley fern,
And the cormorant dives from the Druid's stone.
Now to the archipelago of upland rocks
The animals swim; foxhound and fox,
Rabbit and weasel, cow and sheep,
Skulk in the bracken or climb the steep
Steps that lead to the summits, crying with fear,
But hunting or hiding from the hunter no more.
The smaller birds, redstart and twite
Fly in short scallops with wavering flight
Over the edge of the tide; starlings and rooks
Swarm like gnats around the heads of the peaks,
And the raven high above the rest
Sees the foraging waters reach his nest
And caws like a foghorn to the roaring west.

And now the tall waves bound
Over the mountain tops. The animals are drowned
Where they crouch; the birds fly
Till they drop. The sky
Is black as a coal-pit, and the breaking moon
Spreads in a belt of smoke and dusty rain.
With a gravelly hail of flying shale
Stretched behind like a comet's tail.
It bursts as if charged with dynamite, is whirled
In closing spirals, and the fragments hurled
Down to the dark equator of the world.

IV

As the new moon drops into the sky
And hangs for the first time on the pull of the earth,
Old Tyson steps on to Scawfell Pike.
The waterfalls flow off; the sun shines
On the cliffs which lift like whales in the sinking sea;
The long lakes dammed in the scoop of the dales
Shrink and settle, and the mists simmer. Tyson walks
To the steep fells that slant to the shore
And gazes at the sky. There, as the fogs thicken.
The cloud is formed, and in the cloud
Is set the rainbow.
And Tyson raises his eyes beyond the perspectives of the sea,
    saying:

'Let the sun rejoice with the sun spurge, an herb running with
    milk like the loving kindness of the Lord.
Let the moon rejoice with the moon daisy, which was a delight
    to children in the meadows when the floods flowed back.

Let the stars rejoice with the starfish. Praise the Lord for the
  recurrence of the tides.
Let the earth rejoice with the earth-apple, the potato, a
  sustainer of men in times of famine.
Let the sky rejoice with the skylark, which was the first voice
  to sing above the floods.
Let the clouds rejoice with the cloudberry, which was food for
  the birds as the water sank.
Let the sea rejoice with the seaweed which has taken the water
  as an inheritance.

For the rainbow is the covenant of the Lord set that man may
  see it.
For the seven colours of the rainbow are the virtues of man
  shown that he may remember them.
For red is faith, the colour of pimpernel.
For orange is hope, the colour of marigold.
For yellow is charity, the colour of lady's bedstraw.
For green is temperance, the colour of marram grass.
For blue is prudence, the colour of chicory.
For indigo is justice, the colour of bladderwrack.
For violet is fortitude, the colour of deadly nightshade.
For white is the colour of purity and of the Star of Bethlehem.
And white is the colour of all colours.
And white is the colour of the attributes of the Lord, which we
  cannot understand.
And the white rainbow is the curve of the plan of the Lord.'

> The moon hangs high in the bright sky,
> The bow fades in the cloud, the mist
> Rises like thanksgiving, the sea returns to its routine,
> And Tyson buckles his horse to the shafts of the plough.

[111]

ROCK FACE

(1948)

Rock Face

In the quarry
I found the face – brow and nose and eyes
Cleft in a stare of ten-year-old surprise,
With slate lids slid backwards, grass and plantain
Tufted in ear and nostril, and an ooze
Like drip from marble mouth that spews
Into the carved trough of a city fountain.
Now the rock is blasted, and the dub
Chock-full of soil and rubble, and the shale
Carried away in cart and lorry,
Yet still like cracked reflections in a pool,
Or image broken in a smithereen of mirrors,
Or picture jigged and sawn with paste and scissors,
The rock face, temple, mouth and all,
Peers bleakly at me from this dry-stone wall.

The Land Under the Ice

First in the winter snow falls in the hills,
    Feathers the tops, and roosts like flocks
    Of wild sea pigeons on the sills
And ledges of the blue bluff of the rocks.

And frost lays level bone across the tarns;
    The birds are blizzards in the air;
    The snow takes flesh and hugs the cairns,
A growling mammal huddled in white fur.

The white fur moults beneath the April sun,
    By the black peat where the sykes run;
    And whiter than the hair of snow,
The starry saxifrage begins to grow.

The thin sykes wriggle in the April light,
    Between the granite's grudging thighs,
    The shaggy tails of ferns, the bright
And wary bird-eyes of the bilberries.

The Statesman from the dalehead herds his sheep,
    Gimmer and lambs, to summer heaf;
    And when the scraggy oats are ripe,
By walls of purple cobble piles the sheaf.

But when December mists skulk in pikes,
    The snow holds out its bear-like paws;
    The bracken withers in the claws,
And dead stones skid along the rotting rocks.

And even in the spring the claws cling on
  Clamped tight about the scar's bare edge;
  Nor can the coaxing of the sun
Raise but the mountain scurvy grass and sedge.

The bears of snow in combes of summer garth
  Lie hulked as icy brutes of bone,
  To forage down the cringing stone
When autumn slips the leashes of the north.

Then wakes the ice, and creaks and heaves its back,
  And shakes the loose screes with its haunches;
  The slender spines of rowans crack,
And splitting stones startle the mountain finches.

The birches splinter beneath pads of snow;
  The gullies grind their grooves below
  Porphyry crags, where fangs of ice
Prize out the hip-bones of the precipice.

Down the dale's wide lobby shepherds flee
  To orchards of the southern shires,
  Leaving the wheel, the scythe, the plough,
And hinges rusting on the gates of byres.

But still the Statesman waits and sees the teeth
  Of the ice gnaw ancestral fields;
  A footstep at a time he yields –
His white beard wagging in the blizzard's breath.

He sees the huge hulk of the wolving snow
  Stalk slowly down the dale, and crush
  The cottage roofs and lintels, push
The funnelled chimneys down, with fore-nails hoe

Up ashes, elms and sycamores, and sliver
  Flagstones from flanks, as thunder-quakers
  Making the hamlets change their acres
To slide along the quartz trail of the river.

And there the angular wild northern ice
  Takes grip upon the shrunken land,
  Creeps down the coast, and builds beyond
White seas of mountains mountains of white seas.

II

The lilac cloud-wrack of an arctic spring
  Skeins through the sky like geese on wing;
  Grass grows in combes, and sphagnum moss,
Hectic with flowers, beyond the reach of ice.

In southern ghylls the Statesman feeds on shoots
  Of alpine cresses, sapped with rain,
  The leaves of creeping willow, roots
And bitter berries of the tundra sun;

Fishes through holes in ice, and hunts the seal
  And legendary arctic bird,
  Of flesh and blubber makes his meal –
Raw blood and feathers glued upon his beard.

Poleward, ten thousand years, the Northern Lights
    Stripe the sky with fiery bars;
    The ice peaks burn in the high nights,
And flakes of darkness float across the stars.

The Statesman climbs the stalagmitic rocks,
    His body tanned like leather, bare
    To the salt wind, his withered sex
Hanging about his haunches like grey hair.

The moonlight smokes around the icy spires;
    The belfries of the fell-tops peal;
    And frost tugs tight his thoughts like wires
That sing and whistle in his hollow skull.

And the bright polar star shines on his brow
    And brands his eyes; his eyelids feel
    The glowing cinders of the snow,
And a white darkness blinds his selfing soul.

III

And now the cautious claws of snow draw back.
    The glaciers dwindle. From the ice
    Chill rillets sweat; a muddy beck
Bursts like a geyser through the dale's wide jaws.

The crags thrust up again, and sides of valleys,
    Planed vertical, where waterfalls
    Pour down from tributary gullies
Left hanging in the air like spouts on walls.

In hollows blocked by glacial drift, the snow
    Melts into tarns and brackish moss;
    And noon by noon the lithe lakes grow
In gutters gouged from out the basalt's base.

Boulders and gravel, clay and mud and sand,
    Are shovelled loose about the land;
    And marsh-grass oozes purple stains
Over the tumuli of low moraines.

Rushes and sedges sow themselves, and clumps
    Of cress, and yellow marigolds
    And water-lilies in the sumps,
And buttercups in flood in the wet fields;

Grass of Parnassus, with wax Spanish combs
    Which the green scum of duckweed smirches,
    Devil's-bit scabious with mauve domes,
And aluminium saplings of the birches.

Back goes the Statesman to his birth-right land
    Under the crag's new gable-end,
    And sees the chipped and chiselled stone,
A landscape unfamiliar, yet his own.

He gathers boulders and cleft slate and builds
    A hut, a cairn, an intake wall;
    Hunts the wild cattle on the fell
And drives them to his milky-pastured fields.

And catches sheep and herds them into flocks
  And breeds of tups of his own choice,
  Sees fleeces blossom by the rocks,
And at the golden cloud-set lifts his voice: –

'O in the white night of the bone I've heard
The senile north gods howling loud and high;
The wind-god, shrieking like a migrant bird
That drills the carbon blackness of the sky;

The wheeling sun god's drunken midnight groan;
The dawn-god, crowing like a silver cock –
But always in the skull-pit have I known
The silent god within the silent rock.

The snow shall shrivel like an old man's skin,
The blistered leaves drop from the trees like hair,
The rind of soil shall peel and rot within
Till skeletons of Earth and Man are bare.

And ever to the true north of the rock
Is polarized the compass of the bone,
Pointing to time beyond the shifty clock,
Pointing to land beyond the homely stone.'

A Street in Cumberland

The brick wall of the garden doubles
The long folds of the street;
Hydrangeas blow their blue-white bubbles
In plots of soil the size of carpets. Neat
Is the rough-cast, and the doors set back
Deep in the doorways, alternate numbers
Brassed on the boards above the lock –
And not a neighbour now remembers
That the eighth or ninth house from the end
Was not built with the street, but stood a farm
Two hundred years on its own land,
And the rest of the street was shunted firm
Against it when the town was made on the mosses.
Come round to the back and you will find
The old, uncovered walls – slate bosses
Two foot by two, with cobble-ducks for gable-end,
Cemented to a breccia that would stand
Square with its sandstone joints against the high
Blustering of the bragging wind
That skims the beard off the Irish Sea.
Where the cows bent to the stream,
And the sheep-dog looped the sheep,
The gutters drain the water. Yet a dream
Grips at the house when the roofs are asleep,
True to the loins of the rock that bred it. When the slag
Is puddled across the clouds, and curlews fly
Above the chimneys, the walls thrust like a crag
Through the dark tide of haematite in the night sky.

December Song

On the eaves
A robin sings, with berry eyes
And breast redder than the dead leaves
Dangling his notes like beads,
A luminous, tinkling string.
A robin sings in the evening,
Under smoky December skies –
And so would I sing.

In the sky
A star shines on the kerb of day.
The waking night from light-bleared eye
With one clear, glowing tear is weeping,
Dipping its lids to mine.
A star shines in the dusk,
Not frosted yet by the Milky Way –
And so would I shine.

Winter Song

The blowing clouds are blue of face.
   Dark skeletons of trees
     Are fleshed with snow.
     The sky sags low;
   The bramble's tagged with lace,
   And snuffly gutters freeze.

Come, blizzard, block my sight and black it,
   And freeze my creaking blood.
     Let heel and hand
     As scarecrow stand
   Wrapped in an ermine jacket,
   A stoat's coat round the wood.

But still the berries have no rest,
   The aching seedlets start
     Once more to grow,
     And fingers know
   Beneath the icy breast
   The warm roots of the heart.

Snow Song

Lay the yellow jasmine
On the blue snow;
Let the berries of the yew
Fall through white shadow,
Pitting the skin
As raindrops do.

Now let all colours
Be simple as day –
The blue and the yellow,
The green and the grey,
And the complexity of light,
Simpler still than they.

And while the heart
Lies under snow,
Let the will write
Its elemental rainbow:
Green is green and white is white,
However brown the world may grow.

Frost Flowers

The air is solid, now, as glass:
Through it dawn and graylight pass,
But Body, like a kept-in child,
Presses its nose against the cold,
And the dim windowpane denies
Knowledge and sense to all but Eyes.
Now slowly seeping from the east
The anaesthetic of the frost
Spreads across the road's long throat.
The soil is white as winter stoat,
The roofs are padded with white felt,
Chimneys are Lot's wives of salt,
And smoke stands stiffly in no breeze
Like snowy ghosts of trunks of trees.
There's not a movement, not a sound
Above the hibernating ground.
But from my freestone window-sill
Summer flowers are sprouting still:
Seaholly, thistle, blackthorn, whin,
Juniper, butcher's broom and pine,
Herb and conifer and shrub
Sprung in the night from a red dub,
All stemmed and sapped with the cold ice,
And hung with webs of broken glass,
Jagged as a hedgehog's jaw
And spiked against the nibbling thaw.
So in the winter frost fronds rise
Across the pupils of my eyes,
For the live skull's a flower-pot

That's nurtured more by cold than heat,
And the mind's saxifrages grow
To stringent coaxing of the snow.
Turn, then, the face to the cold north,
To the green sky and the white earth,
Where frost is nutmeg to the tongue,
Coltsfoot to the coughing lung.
And let the Eyes stretch out beyond
Horizons of the yellow hand
To where beneath the North Star roll
The Arctic Circles of the soul.

Early March

We did not expect this; we were not ready for this –
To find the unpredicted spring
Sprung open like a broken trap. The sky
Unfolds like an arum leaf; the bare
Trees unfurl like fronds of fern;
The birds are scattered along the air;
Celandines and cresses prick pinpoints white and yellow,
And the snow is stripped from the fells.
We were not prepared for this. We knew
That the avalanche of war breaks boundaries like birches,
That terror bursts round our roofs; we were aware
Of the soft cough of death in the waiting lungs. But this
Has caught us half-asleep. We had never thought of this.

The Burning Rose

(A Poem for Lady Day)

Above the golden crocus climbs the rose,
   The rose that is the world's flesh and our own,
Rolled inward, folded, foliated close,
   The red bud rocking on the bright green bone.

The calyx flickers hairy fire, the tight
   Petals are frayed with flame and burn like coal;
The wicks of stamens flower into light
   And leave the shy flesh smouldering, but whole.

Millom Cricket Field

The soft mouths of summer bite at the eyes,
Toothless as a rose and red as the ragged robin;
    Mouths on lip
    Rouse to sleep
And the green of the field reflected in the skies.

The elder-flower curls inward to a dream,
And memories swarm as a halo of midges;
    Children on the grass,
    Wicket-high, pass,
In bue sailor jackets and jerseys brown and cream.

Among the champion, legendary men
I see my childhood roll like a cricket-ball.
    To watch that boy
    Is now my joy –
That he could watch me not was *his* joy then.

August

Here the tide of summer thrusts its last
Wave, and ebbs, and leaves the white foam stranded
Among the weeds and wagons – white flowers of foam,
Wild carrot and mayweed. The sandstone wall
Dribbles with hanging plants, and the slant of the embankment
Is tousled and tussocked with grass. Up tall
Turrets of sorrel the bindweed climbs
Like a spiral staircase, and cinders from the railway
Drift in the one white bell that swings from the top.
Bramble claws among the sleepers, and its ruff of petals
Slips from the green berry, and grass and flower and weed,
Topheavy now with seed, are tired and bent.
The fists of the blooms unclinch and let the fruit
Fall from the palm of the hand. And we, in a season of work,
Close our eyes, nor count the crown of our labours,
But wait while dark pods form in the brain,
And fingers ripen in the drowse of autumn.

St Luke's Summer

The low sun leans across the slanting field,
And every blade of grass is striped with shine
And casts its shadow on the blade behind,
And dandelion clocks are held
Like small balloons of light above the ground.

Beside the trellis of the bowling green
The poppy shakes its pepper-box of seed;
Groundsel feathers flutter down;
Roses exhausted by the thrust of summer
Lose grip and fall; the wire is twined with weed.

The soul, too, has its brown October days –
The fancy run to seed and dry as stone,
Rags and wisps of words blown through the mind;
And yet, while dead leaves clog the eyes,
Never-predicted poetry is sown.

Tyrus

From the city strong in the sea, the city of the islands,
Inhabited of seafaring men, the fleets sailed out
On the swell of the tide down the wide channel,
Their mainmasts half as high as the mountains which they
    passed.
The raven flew among the gulls, and the mist from the fells
Was bloomed with salt from the breath of the sea.
The ships sailed far into favouring oceans,
Knew the wild harbours but held none for home,
Bone and breed of many shores – for once their hulls
Lay red and amorphous in a frozen plain,
While upside-down the masts grew green on a burning hill.
On the deck the passengers walked or leaned against the rails.
Gazing at the city strong among the mountains,
Fair men and dark, steep-browed and slant, speaking
The cosmopolitan dialect of the islands;
And the ships sailed till the dunes sank in the sea,
And the mountains floated in the fog, and the city was
    forgotten,
And dinner was served below deck.
The men trafficked among the long continents
Buying steel, wheat, wool, furs, beef and hides,
For commerce with the city, but a shout went up
That never reached the ears of the bargaining harbours,
A shout went up from the women and a cry from the children
And the city itself roared like a breaking rock
And the islands shook at the sound of its fall.
The fishermen now come in their little boats,
Old bearded men with ear-rings, and spread their nets

Where at low tide the pinnacles and towers,
Jagged with mussels, jut through the water.
They remember a tale of the lost years told in boyhood,
How the fathers of the grandfathers of the race
Came from the diddering islands in great ships
And stood by the shore, throwing their cloaks on the water
And wailing to the waves, saying: What city is like Tyrus,
Like the destroyed in the midst of the sea?

Naaman

So this is the river! Cold and still as steel,
Curved round the banks and boulders. Small cascades
Are bent like blades of ploughs and stand as stiffly.
Unceasing movement now is grey and steady
As the dead stone. The roots of thorns
Are plated with the wetness, and lichens nailed
On the rocks like lead. There's not a clipping,
Even, of a ragwort's faded hair
Left in this winter water. This is the river;
This is where I've come! For days I travelled
With my bones groaning at the ruts in the road
And the pain gnawing them. Then from a hut,
A pile of slates half-tumbled into scree,
A lad came out, a red-haired lout,
Chewing a stalk of dry brown grass. He said
The old man said for me to please
Wash my hands in the river. That was all.
He went off spitting the grass into the mud.
So here I am. This is the river. I would have climbed
The highest mountain with the knuckles of my knees
Grinding like a pestle in their sockets. I would have knelt
Hour after hour, my forehead spliced with prayer,
My hands holding my skull. Are not the lowland streams
Wider and purer and cleaner? Would not the tap
Give a better lather than this rocky gutter? I was a fool
To come – let me be fully a fool.
Let the old man have his way, and I'll return

With a bitter shell of scorn to guard my pain.
It's slippery here. The water's in my boots.
Damn boots and water. Come, boy, give me a towel.

Caedmon

Above me the abbey, grey arches on the cliff,
The lights lit in the nave, pale prayers against the night,
For still the Blessed Hilda burns like a brand
Among the black thorns, the thickets of darkness,
The ways and walls of a wild land,
Where the spade grates on stone, on the grappling gorse,
And the Norse gods clamber on the Christian crosses.
Below me the sea, the angry, the hungered,
Gnashing the grey chalk, grinding the cobbles.
The snow falls like feathers, the hail like quills,
The sun sets, and the night rises like a sea-mist,
And the fog is in the bones of the drowned. Here fare far out
Mariners and marauders, foragers and fishermen.
Tearing their treasure from the teeth of the waves, from the
    gullet of the gaping shores –
Over the heaped and heaving hills they return to the wistful
    harbours,
The freeman's blood and the sea's salt frozen on the gold.
Honour to warriors and wanderers, honour to the wise,
Honour to kings and kinsmen of kings, honour to councillors,
Honour to priests, honour to pilgrims,
Honour even to minstrels, the many-songed migrants.
But never have I ventured forth, neither on the northern tides,
Nor more than a shin's depth down the steep and staggering
    shore;
I have not roamed with the fighting men nor fired the
    Scotsmen's byres.
Yet I, even I, have heard the angels speak,
I, who never learned the liturgical tongue,

Who cannot read the written revelation,
Walking at night on the shingle, waking at dawn in the straw,
I have seen long spears of lightning lance at my eyes,
And felt the words, pricked out with fire,
Notched in my bones and burning in my body.
The angels crawled like gold lice through my dreams.
By the grey sea, under the grimacing clouds,
I hack and hammer at the handiwork of verse,
Feeling the sting of words, fearing the angels' threats,
Hoping that when the tide is full I may seek my unhaunted
    bed.

Cowper

He walked among the alders. Birds flew down,
And water voles watched by the river shore.
A mist hummed on his eyelids, blurred and brown –
The self-sequestered with himself at war.

The bright psalms were his banners: Sion, Ind,
Siloam, rang like horns down Joshua's plain.
At noon the thunder rambled from his mind –
He felt the sun beneath the Olney rain.

The Tame Hare

She came to him in dreams – her ears
Diddering like antennae, and her eyes
Wide as dark flowers where the dew
Holds and dissolves a purple hoard of shadow.
The thunder clouds crouched back, and the world opened
Tiny and bright as a celandine after rain.
A gentle light was on her, so that he
Who saw the talons in the vetch
Remembered now how buttercup and daisy
Would bounce like springs when a child's foot stepped off
    them.
Oh, but never dared he touch –
Her fur was still electric to the fingers.

Yet of all the beasts blazoned in gilt and blood
In the black-bound missal of his mind,
Pentecostal dove and paschal lamb,
Eagle, lion, serpent, she alone
Lived also in the noon of ducks and sparrows;
And the cleft-mouthed kiss which plugged the night with fever
Was sweetened by a lunch of docks and lettuce.

Thomas Gray in Patterdale

I hold Helvellyn in my fingers, here
Ringed in the glass.* The clouds are still as paint,
And ghylls like tucks along the four-inch fells
Slant into neat diagonals. The lake
Is bright as sixpence; and if the wind
Bend back the bracken, it is but as hands
Rub shadows into plush against the pile.
There's not a breath of word or air or water
To blur the picture at the mirror's mouth.
But outside the glass
The breeze moves like a man; October trees
Scatter charred manuscripts; the sun
Includes me in its practice – I become
Part of a landscape that I cannot view,
And under the numbers of the wind I hear
        Melodramatic crags and frantic thorns
Whispering simple names I almost know.
What if I listen? What if I learn?
What if I break the glass and turn
And face the objective lake and see
The wide-eyed stranger sky-line look at *me*?

* i.e. a Claude-glass – a small convex mirror in which
it was possible to see the landscape whole and in perspective.

[141]

For Emily Brontë

Snow is not cold, nor soft, nor white,
But gold as steel when the earth's husk
Blossoms like blackthorn in the bright
Blood-streaming sun of winter dusk.

Over the moors walk trees of bone
Re-fleshed in leprosy of snow.
Leaf rots to mould, and wood to stone,
And with the thaw the dear limbs go.

And with the thaw the bodies die,
And ghosts crack green on every tree;
The dead wood burns to the mild sky;
The snow beds lonely in the sea.

Above Ullswater

Two days of sun –
A valley in grey rocks of rain.
And what remains
When the hour-old past flies off like a cloudy comet?
What remains, now, in the world
Of stone and flower, the world
That hand and eyesight know? –

The spore-box of the moss you showed me,
Pulling away its hairy candle-snuffers;
Lichen green as copper salt; the bird
That turned into a stone. These remain
Because they are transient as tides; these remain
Because to the world of fingers they'll come again –
It is the eternal that never stays.

Oh but you
To whom the angels speak in colours,
Was the silence singing, and the shining air
Snowy with angels' feathers?

The stones are hard beneath my feet; the water
Clinks its little teaspoons in the beck;
The world that *I* belong to nudges back again.
But still your hair is trembling in the draught of angels' wings,
And paradisal colours are rising in your eyes.

New Year's Eve

All our perceiving is a memory.
The flood-waters of the senses back sluggishly up the nerves,
And when the waves clamber on the rocks, the upper pools
Are still as goldfish bowls, the weed spread wide on the floor:
But brine chills the blood of the stream, the cool
Frill of foam pushes among the rushes
When the tide is already ebbing from the shore.

The glance is seen
Only when the glance has been;
The touch is felt
Only when the hand is gone;
The word is heard
Only when the word is spoken;
And only when the silence is broken
Is the silence heard or felt or even known.

All our memory is a perceiving.
Only in memory are the seven words
Linked from lip to ear at the heart's call;
Only in memory are the seven notes
Strung on the thread of a tune;
Only in memory are the smile, and all
The accessories of greeting and of parting,
The flush, the wind-unravelled curl,
The round of breast and thigh,
The blue of a dress, the angle of an eye,
The unasked, unintended pressure of the turn of a knee,
Fleshed and embodied as a girl.

To know is to accept that understanding
Is beyond our hands and away from our eyes.
Even a tree is a thought, a girl's hair
Is a creed, a need is a prayer.
Life is faith, seeing is believing:
All our memory is a perceiving.

To a Child Before Birth

This summer is your perfect summer. Never will the skies
So stretched and strident be with blue
As these you do not see; never will the birds surprise
With such light flukes the ferns and fences
As these you do not hear. This year the may
Smells like rum-butter, and day by day
The petals slip from the cups like lover's hands,
Tender and tired and satisfied. This year the haws
Will form as your fingers form, and when in August
The sun first stings your eyes,
The fruit will be red as brick and free to the throstles.
Oh but next year the may
Will have its old smell of plague about it; next year
The songs of the birds be selfish, the skies have rain;
Next year the apples will be tart again.
But do not always grieve
For the unseen summer. Perfection is not the land you leave,
It is the pole you measure from; it gives
Geography to your ways and wanderings.
What is your perfection is another's pain;
And because she in impossible season loves
So in her blood for you the bright bird sings.

Grass of Parnassus

The lake is restless as a lover; black,
Green and sheened like oil.
Wet bracken kindles slowly and the brown, charred hills
Hang from the sky like canvas, swaying through the mist.
The water fidgets in the sedge, the bog
Asphodel is rose-hip-red and bitter,
And the landscape flows and swirls like autumn rain.

The heart is restless too:
In the blood's equinox the body rocks,
And a gale blows along the limbs,
Till hands held before the face are scarcely seen.
Yet still in the nook of love the flower lies,
Brittle and metallic, white, and veined
Like the iris of an eye –
Perfect as a birth beneath the catastrophic sky.

Song by an Estuary

If the wind dints the pool
Like a hand pressed on flesh;
If the gull crimps the sand
With three-twigged feet; if the cool
Tides of light ebb back from the eyes,
And the land is grey as the sea and the sea is brown
   as the land;

If the sand eddies and ripples,
And a brown wave breaks
In a shake of crabs and celluloid;
If the dry sea topples
Over the void of the skyline,
And the mud sucks at the sea-weed's nipples;

If the shelducks blow and bell
Over the graves of the guides,
Long drowned in sand,
When time is empty as a drained shell,
Oh let the tides of the sky, the tides
Of the heart, flow up the shores,
Filling the moment as a fog of stars
Poured in a basin of rock,
That the wrack of days, the thrice-twenty-
Times dry and aching month
Be flooded by this hour's bright plenty.

The Crocus

The winter night is round me like a skull,
Hollow and black, and time has rotted off;
The sky is void, the starry creeds are null,
And death is at the throat in a soft cough.

And rooted in the leaf-mould of the brain,
I see the crocus burn, sudden as spring,
Yet not of seasons, not of sun or rain,
Bright as a ghost in the skull's scaffolding.

It is not hope, this flower, nor love its light.
It makes the darkness glow, the silence chime;
Its life gives sense to death, names black with white –
The timeless flame that is the wick of time.

The Megaliths

Heedless, unheeded of the years they stand;
The rain drips off their chins and lichens spread
A moist green skin along each stony hand
That gropes among the bones of the grey dead.

They did not see the forests flow and fall –
Juniper's blue wave by the fellside shore –
Nor barley batten by the coddling wall,
Nor purple ploughland swipe across the moor.

They hold death in them. Skulls have moulded ears
That deaf remain to curlew, crow and dove.
The human winds blow past them; each one fears
The hoarded ache of a malignant love.

Horoscope

Between the medieval roofs we see
The gold sun's royal progress through the sky;
The state, the prince, the governor is he,
Sovereign of the heaven's autocracy.

Accommodated to the human seeing,
Our small political designs explain
The metaphysical steel cogs of being
Where angels rule the stars and stars rule men.

What angel knows the sequence we began?
What stars depict our destiny above?
What planets dint a constellation's plan
To parallel a meeting and a love?

At the astrologer's device we laugh,
But the absurdity's persistent still –
Only by love we ape a planet's graph,
Only by love we learn an angel's will.

Songs Unheard

I

Dull is the Lenten moon
Like a breathed-on glass above the night,
As from my window, looking down
On streets and chimneys of the town,
I see girls wandering through the brown
Blundering mist –
Blind-man's-buff in the drizzling light.

When the mist held me tight,
Blind I was and bound my eyes
And ears were deaf to the sweet street lies.
And the brain asks the blood,
And the blood replies:
'I could have given you sight' –
But still I wonder if the blood is right.

Under the roofs in the glimmering rain
Shadows of lane and gate and door
Say again the same meant lies,
The same sincere hypocrisies.
And the blood asks the brain,
And the brain replies:
'Sight is a blinder blindness than before' –
But still I wonder if the brain is wrong.

Among the cloudy garden walls
The willows strain beneath the rain;
Smoke like a sea-fret falls
On green streets mossy with the dark.
Oh could I find the truth the lie denies
And in denying pries
Under the shell of the self's self-righteousness.
The Lenten night is calm,
And smoke from the chimneys drifts
On unseen pollen of Palm Sunday palm.

II

Over the dyke the tide of Easter breaks,
Foaming in orchards, froth-deep to the knees;
The yellow willows toss their scurfy locks,
And cherry bubbles bounce on rocking trees.

The longing bees forsake the pollened hair,
And swarm now on the fruit of the ripe breast;
Out of the mouth the curling kisses flower –
But blossoms fade and bees go hive to rest.

And to the bees unknown, the heart that shares
(Knowledgeless still in knowing) their high moan,
And makes the prattling petals pout, endures
Longer than memory and hard as bone.

Pendulum Poem

Leaves fall.
The air is full
Of the fall of the leaves.
The spouts in the eaves
Choke with elm,
Ash, oak
And maple shavings.
The yellow rain
Seeps to the drain
Down the white wall,
Whitewash and white
Smooth-cast and plaster.
The last leaves
Leave the tall
Bare sycamore
And lie on the iron
Rails of the square
Where rust is brown
As a young girl's hair.
The leaves lie
Over the eyes,
Moist yellow eyelids
Blear the light,
Blind the skies.
November fires
Burn in gardens
And Martinmas turns
Oak and ash
To ash and smoke.

The charred leaves
Float in the air;
And soot is sharp
On the dry tongue.
Bright memories
Fall through the mind:
The yellow carpels
Of a flowering youth.
And hand on hand,
Or mouth on mouth,
Find falling leaves
Brittle on fingers,
Dry on the teeth.
In the after-evening
The leaves fall
Slowly as snow,
And bury the night
Under yellow drifts
In the lamp light.

The Swords of Flame

The sky is dark, and brown the clouded sun;
The smouldering of October dims the trees –
Yet in the forest summer's never done,
And the big-breasted foxgloves bride the breeze.

Oh! but the bracken's burning: swords of flame
Flash from each frond of fern and leaf of oak
And gash my loins; my tongue forgets its name;
My eyes are blinded by the bitter smoke.

Song for a Play

Like earth-shine on the moon,
When the moon's a neon wire
Fired by the shock of the sun,
I saw my love in your eyes shine.

I saw my love in your cheeks glow
As the memory of your face
Raced through the daydreams of day
And daylight was a night-light to the moon's dark way.

When night is bandaged round my pain
The full-faced moon is raised,
Brazen in the breath of the sun,
And lights my sleep with the light of a love unseen.

And you from the moon's bright noon
May see the sickle earth
Girthed in a cord of shine,
Reflected by your eyes from the hidden sun.

The River of Flesh

The river of flesh flows white and smooth
Under the crags, under the swill of willows,
Where dreams hang like spider-webs milled with rain.
The river of flesh flows sweetly down the bed of the bone:
But oh do not cry to the lonely sky
Asking why blood should be water and heart a stone –
The river herself has formed the stone,
Tenderly breaking the rock through centuries of pain,
Rolling it like an egg in the nest of her womb.
The stone beats with the slow pulse of the seasons;
The heart of the stone is warm as wood.
The river of flesh flows gently from head to foot,
And light ripples on the waves, the nippled eddies,
The golden water-weeds of hair. Here,
On this shore of tiredness, floats one leaf,
One bright leaf and a berry of the rowan,
A capsule of sun, distilled from the fire of the trees.

The Anatomy of Desire

The anatomy of desire
Is not a living thing
Like blood in arm
Or sap in stem;
Not from the shouldering bone
Do love's limbs hang,
Nor the wooden skeleton
Of sleep-walking tree.

The anatomy of desire
Is not like fire –
Insensate spirit
Swift as a wish.
Flowers of flame
Unbud in a glim
Of crimson, a simmer
Of smouldering down: –
Florescence of trumpets,
Rays, globes,
Thistle-head and mussel-shell
Lobes, that blaze
With filamented stamens
And sparks of pollen
Under the heavy
White hawthorn of the skies; –
Weeds of no root
With flint for seed,
Cinders for fruit,
That shoot in a gush

Of burning green
When what has been
Becomes what is,
When tree turns to ash,
And flesh to ghost,
In the flash and recoil
Of the volleys of change,
The bursting blossoms
Of the volatile soil.

Flesh flowers
And flower burns
And fire returns
To bone and ash;
Ash and bone
Are broken, ground
To worm-bread, worm-cast.
When the soil is cut
Like a festering wound
From the earth's breast,
Earth's heart is shown –
A cold round stone.
Earth's heart is bare,
And no fire glows
Nor flower grows there,
Where adolescent ages
Of herb and hair
Are frozen, soldered,
Tombed in stone.
Only the rain
Soaks in the grain
Leaving the stain
Of a wet winter sunset

Above smoky dunes;
Only the wind
With cat's-tongue breath
Weathers and worries
Stone and air together.

In autumn the mist is brown as the turned earth;
Pimpernel and speedwell sparkle in the soil,
Blear-eyed before evening. Barbed wire
Is tangled thick as witch's broom in birches.
Thistles the colour of string have split their feather pillows,
And grandad beards of sheep's wool wag on the thorns.
The stone lies among straw, cow-dung and cartwheels,
And dust spreads like a crust over blind eyes.
Lichens hatch out – a green or rusty smudge,
Like acid burns, or a dried gob of phlegm;
And then the cuticle grows up the nail,
And roots corrode and probe, breaking, dissolving the stone,
Till a new dust is ploughed in the bone-dry soil.
And now the heart of Silurian ferns
Burns again in foxglove and fireweed,
Fir-cone and briar.
The anatomy of desire
Is only a stone.

The Candle

Poetry is not an end.*
The flame is where the candle turns
To smoke, solid to air,
Life to death, or say,
To that which still is life in another way.
The flame is not an aim,
Nor the brightest light
Any justification for its burning.

The beloved is not love,
Nor poetry the grammar and the theme.
But when the beloved – oh with hair
Like seaweed on the rocks
When desire flows back at the turn of the night –
Then she seems
All that love is
And being herself is loving. So the song
Seems cause and crown of singing, and the dream
The body and bride of longing,
To one who seeks thought's lips with his tongue.

The flame is the poem,
And the light shines little time,
And the poet follows the rhyme into the darkness
And learns there his new, unspoken name.

* This phrase, together with the theme and the imagery of
the first stanza, were suggested to me by Miss Kathleen Raine.

Song at Night

'Music for a while'
Make audible the smile
    That eyes no longer see;
With crying crayon write
Across the unhearing night
    The shape of sighs for me.

Music for a time
Resolve the brawls of rhyme
    That chord within my head;
Sweet as starlight, shine,
Illuminate the line,
    Setting the word unsaid.

When Dryden's page is bare,
And silent Purcell's air,
    And mute the singing sky,
Then let me pluck one name
And echo clear proclaim
    Not I, my dear, not I.

A Second Song at Night

Bangles of stars are jingling
On the black wrists of night;
My flesh is tingling
At touch of naked air;
The sky strips off her light
And clips her to me bare.

Brighter than sun or moon
With peedling, comet eyes
The night bends down,
Bragging her pole-black charms,
And the mad body lies
With Nothing in its arms.

Song From the Songless

No longer tongue and finger
Shape the note or pluck the string;
No longer does my blood know how to sing,
But only remembers now the need and the longing.

Winter, great musician, skald, whose bow
Grinds cello groans from the world's taut soul,
Stretch my sinews, string my nerves
Across the wide gap of the cold,
And let the wind blow, the old
Back-alley gaffer of the north, let the wind blow
Through frozen memories.

         And when the snow
Is cased and plated round the wires,
Let the west wind, the roaring, explorer wind,
Blow through the sockets of my skull,
Scrape out the birds' nests that were once desires,
Scrape out the lichen that was mind,
And sound like a horn above the icy fell.

Or when the wind has gone and the snow shines no more,
Nor icicles hang from the jaw like growing teeth,
Let some casual boy,
Walking where the green sea nabs the shore,
Grubbing among the stones,
Find a white and shining toy,
And rap out his ragtime with my knuckle bones.

Across the Estuary

The fog floats in with the tide and lies on the mosses,
Branching up the channels like the veins on an old man's hand.
The world of field and farm, the woods and the embankment,
Are blurred away like figures on a slate;
Here, under the canvas of the fog,
Is only sand, and the dead, purple turf,
And gulleys in the mud where now the water
Thrusts flabby fingers. The wild geese
Feed beneath the mist, grey and still as sheep,
And cormorants curl black question-marks
Above the threshold of the sea.

Here is the track:
The ruts of cartwheels filled with water, the dark
Brogs of broom. Unseen, a curlew calls –
A shadow slipping through the rippling mist;
Byzantine domes of foam sail up the gutters.
But now – where is the track? where are the ruts? The broom
Skulks back into the dark, and every footstep,
Dug deep in mud, draws water through the heels.
Each step goes wrong. Here, forward – deep, the sand
Shifts under foot like scree. Backward – deeper.
Stand still then – squids of sand
Wrap suckers round my feet. The tide
Tops the rim of the gulleys, and the mist
Tightens its cold, wet nets about my throat.

II

It is not the eyes of the past
That stare through the mist,
But the eyes that belong to now.

It is not the faces of a dream
That bulge through the gloom,
But the faces of the waking sight.

It is not the voices of the dead
That leave the word unsaid,
But the voices of those who live.

III

Thigh-deep in fresh water
I waded the channel
Before the ebb turned.
Do not ask where
Foot first stepped away
From turf to mud,
From dry sand to quicksand;
Oh do not ask where
When foot was bare,
Wings bright in the air
And the sun spinning there,
The wind in my hair,
The unimaginable, rare
Flabbergasting world
Uncurling like a fern,
Unfurling like a flag,
Do not ask where
Foot turned from the ruts,

For my eyes were on the sky
And the wide stripes
Of light above the sea.
And do not ask now
How came I here –
My footsteps veer
Back into the mist,
A bird-track of pools
Oozing like wells
And losing shape
As the sides dissolve.
The past slides
Like sand beneath my feet,
But the past is forgiven –
The unconfessable sins
Of hand and brain and eye,
Murder, rape and lie,
Are washed by the river
To the salvaging brine.
It is not then but now
That tightens like mist about me:
Not how I came
But where I am,
Not what I was,
Nor how I grew
From that to this,
But merely
My being I.

IV

The tide spreads across the marsh; a six-inch rise
Of water covers miles of sedge and plantain;
Gulleys and gutters are confiscated now
Into the grey acreage of the sea; for a while
The inevasible choice of wrong and less wrong
Is forgotten or deferred. The fog
Is rent like calico, and the sun lets down its ropes,
Yellow, frayed and tangled; gulls and sea-pies
Fly up the estuary, shelducks jangle; but
There is no sign of traveller on the flat waters.

In the days when the estuaries of Morecambe Bay and South Cumberland were
crossed regularly by travellers on foot and by coach, the guides marked the track
by planting branches of broom in the sands. This was called 'brogging the sands'.

Silecroft Shore

Beauty is simple
As a stone, smooth,
Worn into one
Movement, the curve
Still as the orbit
A star loops through.

Stone is simple
As bone which hand,
Shoulder or arm
Rims round. Bone
Is smoother than skin,
Rounder than flesh.
Under the teaseled
Mesh of hair
Bone is bare
As thought without words,
Pure as desire
Without image, end
Without world.
Stone is the earth's
Cool skeleton,
And bone the rock
That flesh builds on.

II

I walk among the cobbles by the shore:
Not here the nap of turf, the nibs of marram,
Twiddled like compasses by the wind, describing arcs
On the white sand; not here the rockpools and the sea
Spleenwort and the underwater ferns. Instead,
The shingle grinds its teeth beneath my tread,
The pebbles squeak and squelch as I kick among them,
Dark and wet and salty as mussel shells.
Above the wrack I pick a stone,
Bone-dry, black and bare, no seaweed shavings
Nor barnacles' little volcanoes bursting from its flanks:
An indigo mud-stone, from Skiddaw or Black Combe,
Snapped off the rocks and carried to the sea
In the pockets of the ice, its sides planed flat
To long unequal rhomboids; then
Shaken daily in the dice-box of the surf,
Hammered, filed and sandpapered, its roughnesses are
    rounded,
And what was once a chip, a sliver of slate,
Becomes a whole, self-axelled and self-bounded,
Grained like a bird's-egg and simple as a raindrop,
A molecule of beauty. The sea spurge
Feathers green, dripping sticky sap,
The quick ring-plover shifts and disappears
Like a puddle in the sun, and the stones stay
Perfect and purposeful, acknowledging no way
Other of being than this.

III

I lie along the axis of the world.
  My feet are the poles; the ice
  Chisels my shins; my arms are curled
About the tropics where the mid-ribs splice

The continents together. Naked – though
  Shaggy with larches at the fork –
  I seem, and feel the cold scurf snow
On hair as black as heather in the dark

And hidden armpits of the mountains. Bone
  Splinters along the skyline, bare
  As fortitude, and wind and rain
Gimlet and slice beneath the lathered air.

High from the alps the blood-red rivers fall,
  Veining the snow, and gouging deep
  Canons in granophyr and shale.
As the old miners wrought with feather, stope

And mallet, so the ice and weather crack
  The sockets of the rocks, and boulders
  Chock up the gulleys, and the slates flake,
And what the green ice breaks the grey snow solders.

In warm savannahs of forgetfulness
  The rivers run maroon with blood;
  They flow where brine corrodes my eyes,
And silt the blinded grottoes of my head.

Now brown about my brow settles the mud;
   The Ordovician creatures crawl;
   Across the delta corals spread,
Blooming like rhododendrons; fern and shell

Are stamped in sand like heads on coins. Oh, now
   Heavy the years, the mud; the rain
   Fills, drop by drop, a neapless sea,
And centuries fall slowly, grain by grain.

IV

An old man sat in a waterfall
   And the water dripped through his hair;
His voice was green as a sea-pie's call:
'Come weeds, and turf my skull,
For my hair is loosed by the bite of the beck, –
   Soon my head will be bare;
   I'll have no pride at all.

'Come wagtail, water-ousel sing
   And bubble in my throat;
Come water-rat skulk in my breast,
My flesh shall be your winter coat;
Come water-hen and make your nest
   In hollows of my ribs;
There you'll find a place to play,
For life has rotted my heart away.'

The old man sat in the waterfall
And the water turned his skin to bone.
Stalactites hung from his chin like a beard;
   His shoulders were shelled with stone.
And leaves in autumn drop from tall
Arthritic thorn-trees by the limestone wall
On the old stone man in the waterfall.

V

Bone is simple
As memory, cool
As water that flows
Over jowl and brow
In the pools of sleep;
Drip by drip,
Thoughts bulge and fall
Perfect as the world
Curled about them,
Bent on the water's eyeball. Oh!
From what rains, from what clouds,
From what seas, from what streams
Dribble the ghosts
That flood my dreams?

Memory flows
Cool round the bone,
Glazing the white
Like porcelain. Gaze
On the youthful bone,
That bending spine
And rotting teeth
Made in a cradle.

And the bone says:
'It is not I
That bears the daisy head,
But the limestone generations of the dead.'

Memory is beautiful
As a stone, simple
As a sample of mountain,
A handful of hill.
Oh! cobble on the shore
Can you not remember
What you were before
The valleys were brought low?
Can you not forget
What it is to never know
Rock turning slowly
Back into rock
Long to-days ago?

THE POT GERANIUM
(1954)

The Pot Geranium

Green slated gables clasp the stem of the hill
In the lemony autumn sun; an acid wind
Dissolves the leaf-stalks of back-garden trees,
And chimneys with their fires unlit
Seem yet to puff a yellow smoke of poplars.
Freestone is brown as bark, and the model bakery
That once was a Primitive Methodist Chapel
Lifts its cornice against the sky.
And now, like a flight of racing pigeons
Slipped from their basket in the station yard,
A box-kite rides the air, a square of calico,
Crimson as the cornets of the Royal Temperance Band
When they brass up the wind in marching. The kite
Strains and struggles on its leash, and unseen boys,
In chicken run or allotment or by the side
Of the old quarry full to the gullet with water,
Pay out on their string a rag of dream,
High as the Jubilee flagpole.
                         I turn from the window
(Letting the bobbins of autumn wind up the swallows)
And lie on my bed. The ceiling
Slopes over like a tent, and white walls
Wrap themselves round me, leaving only
A flap for the light to blow through. Thighs and spine
Are clamped to the mattress and looping springs
Twine round my chest and hold me. I feel the air
Move on my face like spiders, see the light
Slide across the plaster; but wind and sun
Are mine no longer, nor have I kite to claim them,

Or string to fish the clouds. But there on a shelf
In the warm corner of my dormer window
A pot geranium flies its bright balloon,
Nor can the festering hot-house of the tropics
Breed a tenser crimson, for this crock of soil,
Six inch deep by four across,
Contains the pattern, the prod and pulse of life,
Complete as the Nile or the Niger.
                    And what need therefore
To stretch for the straining kite? – for kite and flower
Bloom in my room for ever; the light that lifts them
Shines in my own eyes, and my body's warmth
Hatches their red in my veins. It is the Gulf Stream
That rains down the chimney, making the soot spit; it is the
    Trade Wind
That blows in the draught under the bedroom door.
My ways are circumscribed, confined as a limpet
To one small radius of rock; yet
I eat the equator, breathe the sky, and carry
The great white sun in the dirt of my fingernails.

Millom Old Quarry

'They dug ten streets from that there hole,' he said,
'Hard on five hundred houses.' He nodded
Down the set of the quarry and spat in the water
Making a moorhen cock her head
As if a fish had leaped. 'Half the new town
'Came out of yonder – King Street, Queen Street, all
'The houses round the Green as far as the slagbank,
'And Market Street, too, from the Crown allotments
'Up to the Station Yard.' – 'But Market Street's
'Brown freestone,' I said. 'Nobbut the facings;
'We called them the Khaki Houses in the Boer War,
'But they're Cumberland slate at the back.'

I thought of those streets still bearing their royal names
Like the coat-of-arms on a child's Jubilee Mug –
Nonconformist gables sanded with sun
Or branded with burning creeper; a smoke of lilac
Between the blue roofs of closet and coal-house:
So much that woman's blood gave sense and shape to
Hacked from this dynamited combe.
The rocks cracked to the pond, and hawthorns fell
In waterfalls of blossom. Shed petals
Patterned the scum like studs on the sole of a boot,
And stiff-legged sparrows skid down screes of gravel.

I saw the town's black generations
Packed in their caves of rock, as mussel or limpet
Washed by the tidal sky; then swept, shovelled
Back in the quarry again, a landslip of lintels
Blocking the gape of the tarn.
The quick turf pushed a green tarpaulin over
All that was mortal in five thousand lives.
Nor did it seem a paradox to one
Who held quarry and query, turf and town,
In the small lock of a recording brain.

Old Main Street, Holborn Hill, Millom

Under the tiered, theatrical night skies
The street is built of canvas: – folded screens
Slung horizontal from the flies,
Where you'd expect a roof; and slanted wings
That as you pass behind them leave the eyes
Unprompted in the darkness. A property staircase leans
Against a door that's a palace or a pub
As the plot demands, and hessian walls hang slack
In the dim wash of the street-lamps. A freestone sill
Pins a parallelogram of brown
Against blurred purple stucco; Virginia creeper dangles down
In clots and fists of shadow; a misty swill
Of smoke and lamp-light smudges the chute of the hill;
But yonder the station sycamores, old as the town,
Still hoist their rigging, taut and bare and black,
Against the slag's perpetual sailor's warning.

This shadow-play, this make-believe,
Has no intention to deceive:
When memory or morning restores the daytime order
To the Plough Inn, the garage, the Institute,
The Spiritualist Room, the licensed grocer's – then
What the full sun reveals is no
More real, more solid than this. Sun and moon,
Slapping the slates with whitewash or wrapping the bell
Of the market-clock like a ham in a mizzle of muslin, try
In their winking way, to show, to tell
Feet and forehead where to come and go,

And where to sleep and where to die –
But a blind man knows his house as well as I.

Night and morning, daylight and darkness, crawl
On window and wall as nasturtiums or winter jasmine,
With inflorescence of colour and leafage of shade.
Shapes and appearance burst and branch and fade;
Clock-time and season fluctuate and fall
Like an organic river pouring from above,
And fingers touch the truth beneath it all:
Beneath the shape, the wall, beneath the wall, the stone,
Beneath the stone, the idea of a stone,
Beneath the idea, the love.

On a Proposed Site for Council Houses, Holborn Hill Ward, Millom Rural District

Many a spring, passing this dyke, I picked the wild cherry,
  Oozing its beads of milk on branches black with soot
That blows on a straight-from-Lancashire wind from the
    furnace beyond the quarry,
  Where the town like a bird-nest of roofs lies tucked at the
  hill's foot.

And often it seemed, in spite of the smoke, in the tang of a
    March morning
(Last autumn's sorrel stiff as straw, umbrella-frames
Of knapweed, cockerels striking their matches, dead grass on
    the bank burning),
  That none here but the spinks had ever made their homes.

But, look! deep in the nap of the grass, in the puckered pockets
    of dockens,
  Drafted in cobbles and concrete, the lines of kitchen and
  hall:
Plan of a farm, built long ago, now leased to the blackbirds
  and brackens,
  Where lives have dripped from the flags like water into the
  soil.

Let voices return, and proud pianos practise trilled crescendos;
  Let plaster out-dazzle the cherry with spill and splash of lime:
But the children's eyes and the china rabbit will stare from the
  casement windows
  At the ghost of a hearth that warmed the lonely bones of
  time.

[185]

Weather Ear

Lying in bed in the dark, I hear the bray
Of the furnace hooter rasping the slates, and say:
'The wind will be in the east, and frost on the nose, today.'

Or when, in the still, small, conscience hours, I hear
The market clock-bell clacking close to my ear:
'A north-west wind from the fell, and the sky-light swilled and
    clear.'

But now when the roofs are sulky as the dead,
With a snuffle and sniff in the gullies, a drip on the lead:
'No wind at all, and the street stone-deaf with a cold in the
    head.'

From Walney Island

This shore looks back to England: two hundred yards
Of tide, and the boats fratching on their leashes
Like dogs that sniff a stranger. An oily fog
Smudges the mud-mark till the screes of slag
Seem floating on the water. Smoke and fog
Wash over crane and derrick, and chimneystacks
Ripple and ruck in the suck and swim of the air
Like fossil trunks of trees in a drowned forest.
Away in the docks the unlaunched hulls of ships
Seem sunk already, lying on the swash bed
With barnacles and algae.
                                        The sea
Flows up the channel, and the insulated eye,
Picking and prodding among old boots and cobbles,
Selects and builds a private landscape – fancy,
Finned like a fish, flashes about an abstract
Underwater world of shapes and shadows,
Where men are only movement, where fire and furnace
Are only highlights, lines and angles. Forms
Lose their function, names soak off the labels,
And upside-down is rightways, while the eye,
Playing at poet with a box of colours,
Daubs its pleasures across the sky.
                                        The tide
Turns and slides back, and banks of mud
Heave up like waking sleepers pushing the sheets aside;
And, linking shore to shore, emerges
A dripping rib of concrete, half bridge, half causeway,
With neither curb nor handrail,

A foot above the water. Bare toes or hobnails,
Gripping among the slime and seaweed, find
A short cut to the cockles or to work.
                                And like a stone
Thrown through a window pane, the path
Smashes the panorama, pricking the pattern, bringing
    back
A human meaning to the scene. Shadows
Are walls again, angles revert to roofs,
And roofs and walls relate themselves to men.
The hunger of a hundred thousand lives
Aches into brick and iron, the pain
Of generations in continual childbirth
Throbs through the squirming smoke, and love and need
Run molten into the cold moulds of time.

Near Widnes

All this is foreign as London. Ten feet of green
Laid neat as a rug; seven fat red hens
Bandy with laying; a fence

Of flowering holly, with its bunch-of-grape
Buds of yellow-green that hang straight up
As if the silver-willow sky

Pulled harder than the earth. A row
Of Lombardy poplars, and beyond and over
A landscape flat as a council survey: no

Elevation, square fields painted on paper,
Ruled roads and hedges; here and there
A pithead or a crane or a bare tree

Pencilled like a symbol. The poplars switch their branches,
Flicking the cobwebs from the clouds, embarrassed still,
    unreconciled
To feeling Lancashire about their roots. The clock

Strikes a peculiar hour. But mouth and fingers,
Grass and espalier plum-tree in the garden
Accept the familiar wind – wind that,

Mingling marsh and mountain in the same mist,
Pours out one single syphoning of brine
From Windermere to Wigan. The air

Carries chlorine or fungus or the smell of heather,
Visits the diseased lung or the whole,
Takes tone in throats, vibrates on tongue and larynx

With the same words everyways. All language sounds alike
To birds and God – all dialects, local names,
Pet-nouns and proverbs. Coal-house and cucumber-frame,

Lawn, wall, window, chair,
Repeat the private jokes, but the cosmopolitan air
Is an off-come, a visitor, anywhere,

Blowing breath into bones, colour into eyes,
Dispersing a spray of daylight across the skies,
Making each waking a never-foreseen surprise.

Winter by the Ironworks

On the goose green, on the street, softly as snow
The slagbanks drift, and yellow
As snow, and seeming-permanent also,
Checked and chalked by the frost. Slowly,
Slag-flake and-fall slither and crumble over
Back-garden fences, breaking wire and willow,
Choking gulley and grid. Children (their throats
Smoking with dialect) burrow
Tunnels and runnels of shadow
In the yellow-grey of the slope;
Build slagmen, grope
In the crag-icy iron – as if they did not know
That all this mineral marvel, this H 2 O,
This ferrous fancy-piece, will last no
Longer than spit in the fire at the sun's first coking
Up in the morning. Snow-cap and slide will go
Gallivanting through a goose's gizzard, and slagbanks blow
Away in the woosh of the wind. Water and stone
Are shown here to the eye for no more than a moment
Frozen into pattern, and only memory knows
When the atoms fluke an accidental rose.

Reclining Figure

Draped, unshaped, the slagbanks lie –
A dross of smelting, dead and dry.

Nothing disclosed to heart or eye
Of not-yet-sculpted brow and chin,

Or living limbs that lie within,
Hidden in superfluity.

The man of iron now is dead,
And seagull claws of rain will drag

A slow tarpaulin from the head,
Waking from sleep the man of slag.

He beneath unchimneyed skies
Will open grey, ironic eyes,

And, stretching, feel within his soul
The metal that has made him whole.

On Duddon Marsh

This is the shore, the line dividing
The dry land from the waters, Europe
From the Atlantic; this is the mark
That God laid down on the third day.
Twice a year the high tide sliding,
Unwrapping like a roll of oil-cloth, reaches
The curb of the mud, leaving a dark
Swipe of grease, a scaled-out hay

Of wrack and grass and gutterweed. Then
For full three hundred tides the bare
Turf is unwatered except for rain;
Blown wool is dry as baccy; tins
Glint in the sedge with not a sight of man
For two miles round to drop them there.
But once in spring and once again
In autumn, here's where the sea begins.

On the Lancashire Coast

The rocks crawl down the beach,
Taking a thousand years to move a yard;
The seaweed clogs their flippers; each
(Blind, dumb and yet gregarious) lifts an ear,
Like a bat's ear that measures space by echoes,
To catch the effervescence of the sea
Against a neighbour's ribs and shoulders.
Beside such boulders human life
Seems shorter than the suds of foam
Burst by blowing sand:
And yet these fingers (five
New to the touch of five) that bend
One to another like a lip
To speak a kiss, these hands
Shaping the deaf-mute language of the heart,
These wrists that time will strip
Quicker than it smooths the wrinkles on the stones,
Live with a vertical bright permanence
That cuts through death like a knife.

From a Boat at Coniston

I look into the lake (the lacquered water
Black with the sunset), watching my own face.
Tiny red-ribbed fishes swim
In and out of the nostrils, long-tongued weeds
Lick at the light that oozes down from the surface,
And bubbles rise from the eyes like aerated
Tears shed there in the element of mirrors.
My sight lengthens its focus; sees the sky
Laid level upon the glass, the loud
World of the wind and the map-making clouds and history
Squinting over the rim of the fell. The wind
Lets on the water, paddling like a duck,
And face and cloud are grimaced out
In inch-deep wrinkles of the moving waves.
A blackbird clatters; alder leaves
Make mooring buoys for the water beetles.
I wait for the wind to drop, against hope
Hoping, and against the weather, yet to see
The water empty, the water full of itself,
Free of the sky and the cloud and free of me.

The Boathouse, Bank Ground, Coniston

The walls are solid as lead,
Chip of the Old Man. *
Spiderwebs hang unblown from the niches
Weeks after the spider is dead,
And lichens are stiff as verdigris
On an old copper can.

But the floor is free as a wheel –
A wandering and waiting of water;
Where mating insect boatmen with doubled oars
Row to their flat lagoons,
And the planks clank on the swell
When the wind back-pedals against the shores.

The rag-tailed underwater weeds
Like kites strain on the string,
Crane upward to the light;
Eels of sunshine rip and writhe,
Severed by the current's scythe,
End seeking end among the rocks and reeds.

* Coniston Old Man, noted for its slate quarries.

And a girl in a heckberry frock
Dips her arm in the lake
Till the clouds swim round her fingers. Ragwort and rose,
Wetherlam, weather and the yellowy wind
Pour through her eyes like water in a beck,
Leaving the memory smooth as stone.
Time flows
In and out of the boathouse,
In and out of the mind,
But the now of the self is stiller than the rock.

Canon

Beside the paper-mill at Burneside, Westmorland

I only spoke to see the tree
In flood – I only spoke to see.

I only looked to hear the weir
In song – I only looked to hear.

I listened just to tell the yellow rag – I listened just to tell

The yellow ragtail how to show
And teach the yellow ragwort how

I only came for speech of beech
And beck – I only came for speech.

Scarf Gap, Buttermere

There is no need to describe the track; a pencil
Drawn diagonally across a slate
Would be more precise than words. The stone walls
Lay ladders of grey against the green; the green
Glissades into the lake.
This pass is known, defined and understood
Not by the eyes but by the feet,
The feet of men and sheep that tread it: the young
Teacher from Cleator Moor, pushing a bike
With a burnish of poetry on the rims;
The girl who is soon to bear a foreigner's child;
The lad who leaves the pit shafts of the Solway
To grope for a brighter fire than coal.
These, in the clang and shuffle of the world,
Are shunted along strange, disordered rails,
To crash on viaducts or into buffers
Or bide in sidings where nightshade trails on the lines.
That world they rejected once, perhaps once only,
And scrambled up the screes of the slithering moment
To seek a combe unquarried yet by change,
Where memory, returning with the wheatear,
Could find the name scratched on the same stone.
Therefore to them this dale, this pass,
This double queue of hills, High Stile and Melbreak,
Robinson, Grassmoor and Hobcarton Fell,
(Themselves the wrack and backwash
Of the geological tides) seem now

More lasting memorial than the rubble of cities –
A track that the wild herdwicks still will tread
Long years after the makers of tracks are dead.

Ravenglass Railway Station

The up-line platform bridges a metal road
That slopes unwalled to salt and sand, and boats
Anchored in green-webbed goosefoot and sea aster,
Tarred spars and bendwaters, the cockly trod
Of stumps that mark the ebb-track of the ford.
Here when a blathering, Ulster storm
Chivies in autumn the tide through the bar of the dunes,
Annexing tar and tarmac for the Irish Sea,
Children, waiting for a train, and nosing
End to end of a station long as a Blackpool pier
Can drop their pennies between the wooden planks
Full splash into the water. The storm
Rolls up and over like a drum, leaving
The little auk and the fork-tailed petrel
Brained against telegraph poles; shore-side chimneys
Breathe heavy as horses into the mist; each tree,
Backjacked to the wind, arms high from the shoulder,
Twists in a tatter and tangle of brown
Like a boy pulling his jersey over his head.
Here camped the Romans, sweating in thermal saloons,
Bragging their autobiographies like dice
(A raped virgin beats a burnt town) –
Then in the exilic not-quite-dark, they peedled
Down past the boundary ditch to the huts and the girls,
Warm beds and Welsh voices, while yonder
The dunes, as now, drifted in the purple rain.
Here, too, in the winter of war, the children came,
A Tyneside tang smoking from the stretched larynx,
And here the gold and graphite of the Tate,

Crated and stacked like lemons.
The wagons twitch their toes, the engine blows its nose,
Wheels, rods and pistons bulge and blur in the spray,
And eighty tons of steel float easily away,
Light as suds in the breath of a child. But here
In the fog-sodden fields, under the rain-eaten
Dish-clout of the dykes, among the wrack and rubble
Of the gull-rummaged estuary, or hidden behind
The one-eyed wink of the ticket seller's window – here
Is the root of a race, clamped tight to the rock,
Wringing from the earth its few last drops of green
Long years after the once-tall trunk is down.

The Shape of Clouds

Clouds are not dreams, but dreams
Take the shape of clouds.

Up glass stems of air
The steaming saps rise
To bloom as cumulus:
Meadowsweet and white
Elderflower and may.

Turned like cups of clay,
Pummelled and thumbed by the wind,
Like bubbles bent on a sigh,
They stream along the air.

Every breath we draw
Modifies the sky, adjusts
Temperature and pressure,
Shapes and directs the clouds,
And the warm draught from a kitchen fire
Stirs its spoon among the stars.

The shape we see
Is a shape we dream,
Forming a firmament
In retina and brain;

But the true shape
We neither see nor know –
A barometric order
Beyond the knack of eye,
The gauge of mercury.

Dreams are not clouds, but clouds
Take the shape of dreams.

Rain

Rain
When it falls on land
Is a strange element, owned
By gutters and ponds and pools;
Welcome, yet other,
To buds whose wheels it greases,
Mineral, yet not quite brother,
To dust and stone and sand.
On land we keep account of rain
By watching clouds and hearing the drip in the eaves
And knowing the smell of it among the leaves.

But rain
When it falls on sea
Is scarcely seen or heard or smelt
But only felt –
As if a skelter of birds with pittering feet
Were letting on the glass roof of the waves.
The unsalt water falling through the passive air
Has no identity there
Where each drop tastes of the full Atlantic brine.
Back again in the sea
Rain
Is only sea again.

On Reading the Tide-Table
in a Copy of
The Cumberland Pacquet
for 1793

Waves belong
Not only to the sea,
And not only in the sea
Is the rounding of tides.
For dry above the shingle
The high dunes swell
In a toppling of yellow,
Frothy with marram
At the crest of breaking.

A backcatch of cobbles,
A bubbling of vetch,
And the turf surfs green
Behind the receding wave.
Wire fences stand
Up to the chin in sand,
And twitch by tide
The dry flood swamps the land.

Sand cannot fill the sea,
Nor the sea dissolve the sand;
The waves accumulate,
Mineral, mechanical,
Wet and dry.
And between, in the pebbles, the shy
Shore birds on raffia feet
Flick and fritter,

Piping like piccolos,
And click tails and pass
Clip in the daze of the heat,
Where, transparent as glass,
The air flows through them,
And the piping comes from nowhere.

The Motion of the Earth

A day with sky so wide,
So stripped of cloud, so scrubbed, so vacuumed free
Of dust, that you can see
The earth-line as a curve, can watch the blue
Wrap over the edge, looping round and under,
Making you wonder
Whether the dark has anywhere left to hide.
But the world is slipping away; the polished sky
Gives nothing to grip on; clicked from the knuckle
The marble rolls along the gutter of time –
Earth, star and galaxy
Shifting their place in space.
Noon, sunset, clouds, the equably varying weather,
The diffused light, the illusion of blue,
Conceal each hour a different constellation.
All things are new
Over the sun, but we,
Our eyes on our shoes, go staring
At the asphalt, the gravel, the grass at the roadside, the door-
step, the doodles of snails, the crochet of mortar and lime,
Seeking the seeming familiar, though every stride
Takes us a thousand miles from where we were before.

Gathering Sticks on Sunday

If the man in the moon
Gazing at the waning earth, watches
How the frayed edge of the sunset catches
Thimbles and nodules of rock,
Hachuring distinct with threads of shadow
All that is hammered flat in the earth's brass noon;
And if he sees,
New in the level light, like pock-
marks on a face, dark craters,
The size of acorn cups, or scars
Vast as his own dried oceans, then
He'll know that soon
The living world of men
Will take a lunar look, as dead as slag,
And moon and earth will stare at one another
Like the cold, yellow skulls of child and mother.

The Unseen Centre

They say the moon
Keeps always turned the same face to the earth,
So that her skyward hemisphere,
Throughout the month-long day
Of fortnight dark and fortnight noon,
Stares at the pin-pricked Milky Way
Or the sun eating the fuse of the black year,
But never sees the world
Round which she circles backward. Maybe, we,
Through our interrogating reason, see
Planet and sun and the dust-filtered blue, yet do not know
The unseen centre round which our bodies go.

The Undiscovered Planet

Out on the furthest tether let it run
Its hundred-year-long orbit, cold
As solid mercury, old and dead
Before this world's fermenting bread
Had got a crust to cover it; landscape of lead
Whose purple voes and valleys are
Lit faintly by a sun
No nearer than a measurable star.

No man has seen it; the lensed eye
That pin-points week by week the same patch of sky
Records not even a blur across its pupil; only
The errantry of Saturn, the wry
Retarding of Uranus, speak
Of the pull beyond the pattern:
The unknown is shown
Only by a bend in the known.

The Expanding Universe

The furthest stars recede
Faster than the earth moves,
Almost as fast as light;
The infinite
Adjusts itself to our need.

For far beyond the furthest, where
Light is snatched backward, no
Star leaves echo or shadow
To prove it has ever been there.

And if the universe
Reversed and showed
The colour of its money;
If now unobservable light
Flowed inward, and the skies snowed
A blizzard of galaxies,
The lens of night would burn
Brighter than the focused sun,
And man turn blinded
With white-hot darkness in his eyes.

The Outer Planet
An Allegory

Written for the Patronal Festival of St Matthew's, Northampton

For God, who commanded the light to shine out of darkness, hath shined in our hearts, to give the light of the knowledge of the glory of God, in the face of Jesus Christ.

From the Epistle for the Feast of St Matthew the Apostle.

See here in short the state of man as redeemed. He has a spark of the light and Spirit of God as a supernatural gift of God given into the birth of his soul, to bring forth by degrees a new birth of that life which was lost in Paradise. This holy spark of the divine nature within him has a natural, strong, and almost infinite tendency or reaching after that eternal light and Spirit of God from whence it came forth. It came forth from God, it came out of God, it partaketh of the divine nature, and therefore it is always in a state of tendency and return to God.

William Law, *The Spirit of Prayer*

> *When the dust is blown*
> *The sky is torn;*
> *When the light doubles*
> *A shadow is thrown;*
> *When the amoeba divides*
> *Man is created;*
> *When the atom splits*
> *Love is born.*

In the beginning – in that which we,
Tied to the tail of time, must call a beginning –
The great continuous sun

(Whose Being alone makes nothing, nothing,
Whose light alone makes darkness, dark),
Focusing his beams as through a glass,
Condensed his brightness into one drop. And even as a drop of
    the sea,
Trapped in a winkle shell at the ebb of the tide,
Contains in a single bead the wide Atlantic's
Brine and bacteria, so into one grain
Was bled the fire of the sun,
And spun through the negative void.
                        And far
At the outermost curve of a cold ellipse,
The flames bent inward, curled like fronds of fern,
And turned their backs on the sky.
The flower of the light was hidden in leaf,
Wrapped in a thatch and overlap of green
That flattened and hardened to rock, till the planet swung,
A dead weight of solid metal,
Its long orbit linked to a pin prick sun.

                When the dust settles
                Man is born:
                When love dies
                Man is divided:
                When the light is single,
                When the sky is alive,
                When the atom is in love,
                Man is whole.

Yet still the fire lives at the heart,
Beneath the slag of centuries, beneath volcanoes,
Their nostrils stuffed with ashes.

                          Still

The solar laws compel the dark, and cold
Contracted molecules of murder hold
The bright potentials of a new-born star.
Oh drive deep shafts between these rocks;
Split as with a wedge the dead strata;
Rip the centre out, annihilate the atom,
And let the fire within burn through.

Fossils

In the bones of the rock
The fossils are living,
Crinoid and ammonite;
In the red of the rock
(Sandstone and haematite)
The fossils are moving,
Coiling, crawling,
Aching for the sea.

The rocks are alive,
As a throat with bacteria –
But out of the throat
Comes the voice of the man.
And out of the limestone,
The roar of the sea's motion:
A wave of woodland can
Drown a submerged ocean.
Out of the sandstone,
A dry, wry note,
The whine of the desert;
Out of the slate, the clucking,
The gulping blup of the mud.

In the man of the rock
The fossils are breeding:
Soil receding
Leaves the ribs bare;
Sponges and coral
In a giant ear

Curve and crane
And listen down the hill.

In every wall,
In knuckles and sockets of rock,
In skulls of shale,
In gravel and scree,
Are eyes and eyes,
Tribolite and belemnite,
Staring and straining,
As if light were water,
As if skies were the sea.

The fossils are watching
From quag and quarry,
From step and stone,
Moulding the land,
Shaping our fingers,
Calcium and lime.
In the blood of a hand
The fossils are singing,
The shells unfolding,
The tide-bells chiming,
And the rock is alive in our bone.

The Orphan

Here in a cot of earth I stand –
Earth rails me in on every hand –
Walls of sandstone, walls of slate,
Through which I see as through a gate
The slats of fellside, taut and tall,
That gave the stone to build them all.
Backyards are lying, side by side,
For the sun to open wide,
Lifting the lids of shade until
Pigs of daylight flood and fill
Every gulley, hutch, and hole,
Like molten iron tipped to cool.
The children's washing on the line,
Bubbly with buttons, starched with shine,
Tethered or tied by arm or leg,
Fights to be free of pin and peg.
Kitchen chimneys, cowl and flue,
Raise bars of brick against the blue,
And a tight mesh of wood and wire
Nets my sight from stretching higher
Than where the smoke from breakfast grates
Blooms like a currant-bush, and waits
Till the wind flicks and flakes its leaves
And shakes the pollen on the eaves.

Earth my mother, earth my mould;
Earth the shop in which I'm sold,
Priced at the penn'orth of bronze ore
That's all the wealth my bones can store.

Stone and iron, wood and clay,
Block my eyes from light of day,
As if the bracken-blinkered earth
Grudged the gaze she brought to birth.
Leather-or wooden-clogged, my feet
Limp up the same material street,
Where heart of tree and ore of rock,
Gutter and gable, stone and stock,
Overhang like a dark cave –
The vast interior of the grave.

But the wind still can meet me here –
Beyond the marsh, beyond the pier,
The furnace stewing in its stream,
The tannery by the brackish stream,
The empty ratholes of the mines,
The rusted hoops of railway lines,
Beyond the hills of men and moles,
The wind blows in from two Poles.
See how the glass of the town clock
Gleams like an iceberg; see the rock
Of wall and roof resume again
The slither of a slow moraine –
Till on the glacier of the wind
I skate free from the weathered land,
And watch air's frosty thumb-nails probe
The crooks and crannies of the globe,
Sculpting and shaping, that each place
Wear the cut of its father's face;
Watch a tailor's iron of rain
Smooth out the crinkles in the plain
And hear the rasping files of hail
Grate down the rock to sand and shale.

And now I straddle dodd and dip
Like slack wires on a collier tip –
Royalty-rights in sky and shore:
Solid as earth and free as air.

But, look! the earth is whipped to dust,
The rock is cracked like pastry-crust,
And every thimbleful of sand
Fractured and fissured into wind.
Frantic azaleas of flame
Burst from each speck of flint or foam;
Mountains simmer, and seas boil dry,
And suns volatilize the sky.
Oh what's become of air and earth,
Father and mother, lung and mouth,
The elements that gave me breath
Or spoke a negative to death?
What parents can I call my own
When air is fire and earth is bone?

Five Minutes

'I'm having five minutes,' he said,
Fitting the shelter of the cobble wall
Over his shoulders like a cape. His head
Was wrapped in a cap as green
As the lichened stone he sat on. The winter wind
Whined in the ashes like a saw,
And thorn and briar shook their red
Badges of hip and haw;
The fields were white with smoke of blowing lime;
Rusty iron brackets of sorel stood
In grass grey as the whiskers round an old dog's nose.
'Just five minutes,' he said;
And the next day I heard that he was dead,
Having five minutes to the end of time.

Young Him

'Young him!' – we could never remember his name – we'd say,
And he'd reply: 'Young Nic! Young Tom! Young Ted!';
We bragged of youth for a greeting then, instead
Of patting the head of the weather with Good-morning or Good-
    day.

But youth still felt the ache of the long climb
From the slime to the Piltdown grunt and the Latin tags,
Brunting on our backs up the ladder of time
A bag of bones and rabbit skins and rags.

And he alone took the short cut, never
Telling a word of his prospects or his fears:
Started again from scratch in AD Ever –
Younger than us by fifty million years.

On My Thirty-fifth Birthday

There is no time now for words,
Unless the words have meaning; no time for poetry,
Unless the poem has a purpose; no time for songs,
But songs of work and wild methodical hymns.

There is no time for love,
But love of the world in the one; no time for joy,
But joy that is secreted between shells of pain; no time for hope,
But hope that is fermented in the compost of despair.

No time for you, no time for me;
No time for the bramble-blundering of the bumble bee,
The forty winks with the forty thieves
Under the crab apple tree;
No time for time,
But only for eternity.

Rising Five

'I'm rising five,' he said,
'Not four,' and little coils of hair
Un-clicked themselves upon his head.
His spectacles, brimful of eyes to stare
At me and the meadow, reflected cones of light
Above his toffee-buckled cheeks. He'd been alive
Fifty-six months or perhaps a week more:
                              not four,

But rising five.

Around him in the field the cells of spring
Bubbled and doubled; buds unbuttoned; shoot
And stem shook out the creases from their frills,
And every tree was swilled with green.
It was the season after blossoming,
Before the forming of the fruit:
                              not May,

But rising June.

                              And in the sky
The dust dissected the tangential light:
                              not day,

But rising night;
               not now,
But rising soon.

The new buds push the old leaves from the bough.
We drop our youth behind us like a boy
Throwing away his toffee-wrappers. We never see the flower,
But only the fruit in the flower; never the fruit,
But only the rot in the fruit. We look for the marriage bed
In the baby's cradle, we look for the grave in the bed:

                                        not living,

But rising dead.

The Buzzer

Waking at night in winter, with a south-east wind
Coddling the town in smoke and the marsh smell,
I hear again the paleolithic roar
Of the foundry buzzer, and the dark snuffling air
Scratches and pads the sill.

That buzzer, heard in boyhood, meant that nerves
Had stick-o'-rogered through a sleepless night,
Promising a party, a girl, or an exam.
Now, shop signs itch in the wind. I am
Perked as a single point-light

At the pavement end, dabbing the damp distemper
With twists of window-frame and cord.
Age blocks our senses, builds a wall
To shut us on ourselves, until
The streets are rarely heard,

And watching is deaf as sleep. But, with an east wind,
The night slides backward, down a scree
Of memory, the black walls fall in ruin,
And the buzzer wakes the boy whose bed I lie in,
Whose dubious dream is me.

The Oak Tree

The oak tree thrust its fist
Through the brown-paper wrapping of dry soil,
Letting light into the earth. Its wrist
Was rigged with segs, and stems of ivy
Wound varicose veins around the arm.
It opened its hand and birds flew to the fingers
As falcons to a falconer. A charm
Of chaffinch and linnet made tingle the thumbs of winter,
Spring brought gloves of green,
Summer itched with flies, and autumn
Doled out and dropped its pennies for the squirrels,
And the knuckles were wide to the wind. The lean
Old men goggled from the wood – brown snouts
Peeked from the ferns. Dandelions
Feathered their beards with seeds, and bramble knouts
Whipped their leather thighs, but they never felt them.
They shuffled up to the shins through paddock-stools
    and cow-pats,
And stood in a circle round the tree.
The oldest of them all (his beard
Draggled the ground like a weeping willow)
Touched never a stick, but three
Dropped the tree along the line he measured,
Lopped and topped the branches and ripped the bark off,
Till the wet trunk lay bare as a skinned rabbit. He
Drew out the pith and marrow of the log
And planed it thin as plywood. Shavings
Clog-danced on the cobbles, and yellow sawdust
Pollened the October grass.

He took the wood and bent it
Gently as a surgeon setting a broken bone,
But quick with a crack and a splitting of the spine
It snapped and lay dead in his hands. For a space he held it,
Surprised and sad, then (one arm pointing
Across the field to another tree) he threw it
Into a heaped fire of dead leaves
The men had kindled there. The tossed wood
Fell deep in the damp smoulder, till the slow smoke
Pushed up its fingers, gripping the skirts of the air.
And the hand of the fire was the hand of the living oak.

Cave Drawings

It is not the hunters who draw on the walls of caves,
But the old men, and the lame;
Not those who run in the sun,
But those on whose inner eyelids the die of the light
Has stamped a shape that in the night, the darkness,
Glows with stained-glass colours reflected from the brain.

A fire burns in a cleft, and no one knows
Whether the flames burrow into the shadow
Or the shadows flap about among the flame.
Frayed ropes of smoke
Chafe at a boy's throat,
Making him cough and choke,
But snatching a flint he scratches on the brand-bright rock
Two fore hooves and a lish, live mane,
And there in the crocketty light they seem to move.

For the Bicentenary of Isaac Watts

Died 25th November 1748

Life was a narrow lobby, dark,
Railed in with pain; the windows gave
This side on a padlocked park,
That side on an open grave.

But God looked through the skylight; hell
Was six foot down below the ground.
The cellar had a smoky smell;
The wind had a Mosaic sound.

A voice rang out; the organ pealed
Fit to blow the roof off. Stars
Were stacked in Heaven's harvest field,
And halt and hobbled dragged the cars.

Footnote to Genesis 11, 19, 20

There is no word for bird in the bird's diction,
For man himself has improvized their songs, and man
From his lantern eye, clicked at a flicker of movement,
Projects and colours feather and fantail, tawny and tan.

Or roosts his dreams in the steamy thatch of the rushes,
Sends begging migrant wishes that hesitate on the eaves;
Buttons the bushes with eyes of spink and linnet
That catch a gleam of his own in the dark green doubt of the
leaves.

Yet eyes are there already that he's not invented;
Throstles disregard him in whistles he never can
Learn even to hear. In the avian evening, creatures
That are what man means by bird have their own word for man.

For all Sorts and Conditions

O love of God, God's love, love that alone
Gives hate its meaning, and gives argument
    To men, who out of grief and a rent
    Heart, looking on the world's pain,
    Rend from their hearts belief
In all that lends authority to grief,
Euclidizing one and one and one
    To nowt but a nowt –
Have mercy on all who will not accept Thy mercy,
    Who gouge their eyes out
    Because they cannot see;
    Then call their darkness – *Thee*.

A Garden Enclosed

Hortus Conclusus

Red as old plant pots, tall
As the reach of the scrag-arm creeper,
The bricks of the wall
(Greened and grained with moss)
Bar the yard from the street.
Blue slate flags
Lay cracks of black that cross
In a pattern and puzzle for feet,
And rag-tag tiles,
Up-ended in a row,
Hold soil where daffodils
And *osmunda regalis** grow.

Outside, clouds
Explode and condense again;
The Baptist Chapel steeple shakes
Under a gravel of rain;
The sea regurgitates its dead,
And the horizon breaks
With earth-spouts and water-quakes.

But here where soot and tea-leaves
Fertilize the ferns,
And the pale-green butterfly
Arranges her chess-set of eggs;
Where starlings boil on the eaves,

* The Royal Fern or Bog Onion.

And tits with rubber-coated legs
Wire themselves to the clothes-pegs –
Here let the Holy Child
Eena-meena-mumble words
That make the wild
Wind creep like a sheep-dog.
And let His lifted fingers
Magnetize the feet of birds,
And His bright knees run
Round leaf and latch and dust-bin
Till zinc, rust and window-box shine
      eye to eye with the sun.

A Turn for the Better

'Now I Joseph was walking, and I walked not.'
(Book of James or Protevangelium)

Now I Joseph was walking, and I walked not,
Between the allotments on a December morning.
The clouds were mauve as a crocus, peeling back petals,
And a sparse pollen of snow came parping down
On the bare ground and greenhouse groins and dun
Tight-head chrysanthemums crumpled by the frost.
The cock in the hen-run blustered to its perch
On the lid of the swill bucket, rattled its red
At the fluttering flakes, levered its throat open –
And not a croak creaked out.

                    I looked about me:
The snow was stock-still in the sky like pluckings
Of cottonwool glued on a grocer's window,
And down in the brown of the dyke, a smoky feather
Let on a robin's head, between the black
Glass-ally eyes and the gimlet beak,
And never a flick it gave to shake it off.
Workmen on the electric cable track
Swung picks in the air and held them there, rigid,
Raised bait to mouths and never took a bite.
One, putting up a hand to scratch his head,
Shifted the peak of his cap a couple of inch,
And never scratched. A dead leaf drifting
Hung bracketed against the wire netting
Like a pin caught on a magnet.

                                        For at that minute,
Making was made, history rolled
Backward and forward into time, memory was unfolded
Like a quick discovery, old habits were invented,
Old phrases coined. The tree grew down
Into its sapling self, the sapling into the seed.
Cobbles of wall and slate of rafters
Were cleft and stratified again as rock.
And the rock un-weathered itself a cloud-height higher,
And the sea flowed over it. A brand-new now
Stretched on either hand to then and someday,
Might have and perhaps.
                                        Then suddenly the cock
Coughed up its crow, the robin skittered off,
And the snow fell like a million pound of shillings.
And out in the beginning always of the world
I heard the cry of a child.

Innocents' Day

And Herod said: 'Sup-
posing you had been in my shoes, what would you have
Done different? – I was not thinking of myself. This
Child – whichever number might have come from the hat – could
Scarcely have begun to make trouble for twenty or
Thirty years at least, and by that time
Ten to one I'd be dead and gone. What
Matters is to keep a straight succession none can
Argue about – someone acceptable to the occupying
Power, who nevertheless will enable us to pre-
serve our sense of being a nation,
Belonging and bound to one particular place.
I know my people. They are nomads, only
Squatters here as yet. They have never left the
Wilderness. Wherever in Asia Minor the grass
Seams a dune, or a well greens a wadi, or
Sheep can feed long enough for a tent to be pitched,
There they call home, praying for daily
Manna and a nightly pillar of fire. They are
Chronic exiles; their most-sung psalms look
Back to the time of looking back. They never see
Jerusalem in the here and now, but always long to
Be where they've never been that they may long to
Be where they really are.

                                    If this child had
Lived, they'd have started the same blind trek, prospecting
In sand for their own footsteps. Yes,
Mothers are weeping in the streets of Judea, but still the
Streets are there to weep in. If that child had lived,
Not a stone would have stayed on a stone, nor a brother with
    brother,
Nor would all the Babylons of all the world
Have had water enough to swill away their tears.
                                                    That

I have put a stop to, at the price
Of a two-year crop of children, making
What future observers will undoubtedly judge a
Good bargain with history.'

As Trees Walking

The rough light rasps my eyes.
These that were soft as plums for my fingertips to touch,
Fleshing in pupil-pulp the hard stones of their blindness,
Now have the skin scraped off them. If this is sight,
This jangle and tangle and jumble and jerk,
What's the gain to the seeing? – Only – to be
A rat at a rubbish dump with a cartload of rubble
Tipped on your back, an avalanche of ashes
With neither shape nor sense. They give me an orange:
I feel its roundness, the aromatic
Half-sticky rumples of the rind, the rosette of dry fibre
Where the fruit was snapped from the stalk – the light
Has the even sting of acid. They put a scarf in my hands –
A red scarf as they call it: I feel its animal
Hairiness, kittening and knotting – and the light
Is hot and steady as a gas fire. They hold out a mirror,
Saying: 'Look at yourself, man, look!' and now
The light's not there at all.
                                        When voices speak
They come from nowhere and from no one.
There's nothing in the world I can put a name to;
There's neither here nor there. I cannot recognize
The very hands I feel with – they merge and disappear
In the unintelligible otherness of light.
I have shut my eyes to know where I am,
To find the divide between not-me and me;
I have to be blind again to learn to see.

The boiling slowly dies;
The light lies still.
My fingers teach my eyes.
Day by month by year
I learn the near and far,
The three-point and the four-point
Of triangle and square.
I grope to grip the line
That loops in like a string
The substance of a thing,
The There from the Not-There...
The edge, the rim of the glass
In where the glimmering light
Drips and sets and stands;
The round green glass of apple,
The bulbous brown of pear,
I lift them to my sight
And the colour spills on my hands.

My eye-holes now grow fingers,
My lids stick out their tongues.
Round and smooth is red,
Rough and pointed, green.
And my tongue strokes the pointed,
My fingers chew the smooth,
And seen, seen, seen,
In a new sense of a new sense,
Are damson-leaf and damson,
Water and butter and bread,
Table and chair and bed,
Hearth and home and head,
Seen, seen, seen,
With a new touch of a new tongue,

As if music had a scent,
Or the taste of peppermint
Were a tinkle in the ear.
And all of it early as dew
To my not-mine, not-paid-for,
Experimental view;
For all wives are virgin,
And all eggs fresh-laid,
And every finch a pheasant,
And every pin, new.

The Seven Rocks

FAITH HOPE CHARITY
Fortitude Prudence Justice Temperance

Noi salivam per una pietra fessa
che si moveva d'una e d'altra parte,
sì come l'onda che fugge e s'appressa.
Purgatorio, Canto x, 7–9.

(The Seven Rocks are the seven main types or
groups of rock which form the body of the English
Lake District and of the surrounding parts of
Cumberland, Westmorland and Furness. They are
dealt with in the following poem in the order of
their geological antiquity.)

I

SKIDDAW SLATE
Ordovician

Night falls white as lime; the sky,
Floury with cloud, reflects the rising glow
Of the cumulus of earth. Only
The seaward side of crags, the under-eaves
Of trees, west-looking windows, gates and gables
Unfrilled by snow, hold darkness still:
Elsewhere, the frost precipitates
The once dissolved, dry dregs of day. Heavy
With sediment of shadow, Black Combe stands –
A humped white paradox. The rocks
Are older than the snow, older than the mason ice;
Here the river of time in a delta spread

The bulged and buckled mud that heaves us firm
As faith above the misty minutes. The snow
Covers field and fence as a child's white muffler
Wrapped round the quarried ear. No thorn or scree
Fractures the rim, and the lower hills,
Fleecy as ewes at tupping time,
Lie flocked together. The Celtic tides
Ebb from the marsh and the buck's horn plantain,
And Norse birds breaking their migratory flight
Let on neolithic tombs, levered from the ribs of the rock.
Grey decades
Fade and stain the stone like lichen. The snow
Holds the colour of the seasons
Spinning into white, and time is frozen
To a long, shining icicle of light.

II

SCAFELL ASH
Ordovician – Borrowdale Volcanic Series

The skin of the snow
Breaks and wriggles
From the napes of the fells
Like white snakes;
And blue as gentians
The smooth crags shoot
From green sepals
Of grass and moss.
For now, before
Daffodils light
Like a powder fuse
And damsons whitewash
The orchards of the dale,

[243]

Now is the time
When the rocks flower
High on their stalks,
When the metal sap
Of bracted craters
Unfolds slowly
In porphyry petals.

Hope is not looking
Forward or onward,
Is not of the future.
Only the bone
Can hope; only
The un-closed eye
That learns (still staring)
Never to see.
Therefore hope
Is a theological virtue
And a geological grace,
Felt in the why
And wherefore of a rose,
And when rocks solidify
And the watching sky
Knows the fire's purpose
And the way the water flows.

III

CONISTON FLAG
Silurian

Sunk like a moletrap in the field,
Turfed with ash and poplar, sealed
With bramble, strung with rush and ling,

The quarry snares the early spring.
Tipped with purple at the lip,
Hellebore-green the strata dip
And undulate like tracks of snails
Written in silver on blue walls.
Centuries of river mud
Are combed in stone as grain in wood:
Beech-green, birch-green, holly, grey,
Lichened in pace-egg colours, gay
With cochineal and onion-skin
And rusty bright as an old tin.
Here a slate as hard as steel,
Tubular moulding round the keel
Of plated rock, and here a shale
That flakes and shaves to finger-nail.
The stream divides, the waves obey,
Now charitable in decay;
And children lie in sighing beds –
A river floor above their heads;
Safe in a woad-blue dream each crawls
An Ancient Briton in mud walls.
When it disintegrates the stone
Builds up a capital of its own.
In dormer, porch and gable-ends,
Chimney and windowsill, it blends
Silt of a fossil-time of tides.
Blue stone in every cleavage hides
Brown-sugar crystals, dust of ore,
The sand of that Silurian shore;
With Kirkby Roundheads on the roof
Purple as polyanthus, proof
Against the flocking, mid-March weather,
When the wind's wing and the gull's feather

Fly screaming off the sea together.
Lilac and winter jasmine fall,
Yellow and mauve, on backyard wall,
Dropping their petals on the slate –
Slab paving laid from door to gate;
And the roots' fingers, sopped with rain,
Crumble the stone to mud again.

IV

ESKDALE GRANITE
Igneous intrusion in Old Red Sandstone

Above the dint of dale,
Meadows and mosses, by the side
Of the cat-backed bridge where trailing waterweed
Swivels now to the sea, now to the fell,
At the pass and check of the round-the-corner tide;
Above the salty mire where yellow flags
Unwrap in the late upland-lambing spring;
Above the collar of crags,
The granite pate breaks bare to the sky
Through a tonsure of bracken and bilberry.
The eyes are hollow pots, the ears
Clustered with carbuncles, and in the evening
The warts of stone glow red as pencil ore
Polished to a jewel, and the bronze brow wears
Green fortitude like verdigris beneath a sleet of years.

MOUNTAIN LIMESTONE
Lower Carboniferous

By the Kent Estuary

Out of their shells the sea-beasts creep
    And eels un-reel from holes;
With eyes of stone they stare and weep
    Green stalactites of tears;
    On sea-washed caves of years
The temporal tide reclines and rolls,
And miser mussels, packed and pearled,
Lie like a clutch of peewit's eggs
    In the stone conger's coils,
    Looped around the world.

Where flinty clints are scraped bone-bare
    A whale's ribs glint in the sun.
Coral has built bright islands there,
And birch and juniper fin the fell,
Dark as a trawling under-wave,
With rockrose opening three
Green hands that cup the flower,
And chiselled clean on stone
A spider web of shell,
The thumbprint of the sea.

By the Duddon Estuary

See how the prudent stone,
Secretive sea-beast bone,
Holds, holds in the mould
Rubies and blood-red gold,

Veins of golden blood
Wired below the flood.
Drop by drop the ore
Drips, drips from the shore
Through hollow ribs of rock
Where skeleton fingers lock
Over the paunch of gold
Bladders and blebs of old
Distilled, filtered gold,
As a new penny bright
And red as haematite.
Long-shank diviners stand
Prodding and probing the land,
And steel nebs bore
Down to the hoard of ore;
The coffers of the rock
Spring open at the shock,
And a new life is built upon
The buried treasure of the bone.

VI

MARYPORT COAL
Upper Carboniferous

In Inglewood, in Inglewood,
    The birk was blithe and blue;
The bracken scratched its antlers
    Where the leather trees grew.

Green twigs forked from the horns of deer,
    Red tongues flicked from the flower,
And branches writhed like lizards
    In the wood-beast's bower.

Oh merry it was in the greenwood,
    All on a summer day,
When the crested sun like a burning bird
    Dived through the simmering spray.

The fountains of the plunging ferns
    Poured bright fronds on the ground,
And deep in a wave of boiling green
    The feathered sun was drowned.

And sand flowed over Inglewood,
    The sea rocked green as trees,
And flung a froth of elderflower,
    A fret of blackberries.

Up spake a forest outlaw:
    'Let justice now be done –
Under the waves of Inglewood
    We'll drag for the bones of the sun.'

They dragged deep in the fronded sea,
    Deep in the rocking land;
They hooked the sun at the ebb of the green
    And cast it on the sand.

And buds and bells and spikes of flame
    Flowered from the black bones' side;
And the seed of the sun burned back to the sun
    On the greenwood tide.

VII

ST BEES SANDSTONE
Permian

Across red slabs of rock
I gaze down at the architectural sea. Now
The same sea re-fingers back to sand
That which was made from sand. The stone is grained,
Smooth as walnut turned on a lathe,
Or hollowed in clefts and collars where the pebbles
Shake up and down like marbles in a bottle.
Here the chiselling edges of the waves
Scoop long fluted grooves, and here the spray
Pits and pocks the blocks like rain on snow.
Slowly the rock un-knows itself. The sea
Recoils, winding its springs; the black
Bladderwrack congeals in scabs of blood
About the pools where now the autumnal sky
Cools green and salty. The chalky tideline
Is rubbed out by the duster of the dusk.
The ribbon of life lies lightly on the surface –
The borderline of sky and rock,
Of the space above and the space below, and both
Belong to the wide constituency of death.
As mould on a stone or wrack at the sea's edge
Life spreads its fronds and feelers.
                                    Faith and hope
Are incomprehensible here as a star to a starfish –
Temperance is the one virtue.
                              To wait, accept,
To let the wind blow over, and the sea
Ebb and return, raise and destroy – that
Is the one virtue; only so

Can sky and sea and rock reveal their nature.
The bacillus interprets the sun, and only in life
Can death define its purpose.

                                        The sea
Creeps up the sand and sandstone like a moss;
The crest of the rocks is cracked like a breaking wave,
The land declines again to its old rebirth:
Ashes to ashes, sand to sand.

Part III. Kirkby Roundheads – Round-headed roofing slates from Kirkby-in-Furness.

Part VI. Inglewood. Near Maryport the West Cumberland coalfield touches the edge of the forest which once stretched from the Solway to the Eden. Strictly speaking, Inglewood was in the valleys of the Caldew and the Petteril, but in the Border Ballads (as here) the name was often applied to the whole of the forest area.

NO STAR
ON THE WAY BACK

(1967)

Ballads and Carols

I'll tell you a ballad of Three Wise Men
Who handed their books in at five to ten –
They signed themselves out with a kick of the pen
      And set off to follow a star.

The sky was alight like Bonfire Night,
Their glasses were polished, their purpose was bright,
And their route lay before them lined out in light
      As they set off to follow the star.

The sea flared up like a house on fire,
The wind roared out like a Male Voice Choir,
The sky-writing rocketed higher and higher
      Saying: 'Follow that, follow that star.'

So they set off once more, those Three Wise Men,
They drank in the night-air and never said: 'When',
Turned their backs on the sun and then met it again,
      As they kept on following the star.

They prayed in ones and they talked in twos,
They walked in silence or aired their views,
They walked till their feet wore holes in their shoes,
      As they kept on following the star.

And always their ears were alert for a sign,
At the clink of a bell or the twitch of a line,
Or the voice of an angel – or maybe just mine –
      That still said: 'Follow the star.'

Instructions will be waiting – they stared on every side,
Analysed and classified horizons near and wide,
Explored avenue and alley-way, cul-de-sac and glen,
Where instructions might be waiting for the Three Wise Men.

They watched the shifting of the smoke and diagnosed the skies;
They searched encyclopaedias and called the answers 'Lies',
They numbered bones and cherry-stones and multiplied by ten –
Oh, instructions *must* be waiting for such Three Wise Men.

So put the cake beneath your pillow, blow the candles out in turn,
Keep a count on all your birthdays, carry bits of coal and fern,
For in bus-tickets and feathers or the tea-leaves in the tea
Instructions will be waiting, too, for you, my friends, and me.

Unbutton coats and jackets, take a look inside your heart,
Open all the cupboards, let the skeletons depart,
Peer deeply in your dusty soul and tell me what you see,
For instructions will be waiting *there* for you – and – me.

Shepherd's Carol

Three practical farmers from back of the dale –
    Under the high sky –
On a Saturday night said 'So-long' to their sheep
That were bottom of dyke and fast asleep –
    When the stars came out in the Christmas sky.

They called at the pub for a gill of ale –
    Under the high sky –
And they found in the stable, stacked with the corn,
The latest arrival, newly-born –
    When the stars came out in the Christmas sky.

They forgot their drink, they rubbed their eyes –
    Under the high sky –
They were tough as leather and ripe as a cheese
But they dropped like a ten-year-old down on their knees
    When the stars came out in the Christmas sky.

They ran out in the yard to swap their news –
    Under the high sky –
They pulled off their caps and they roused a cheer
To greet a spring lamb before New Year –
    When the stars came out in the Christmas sky.

Wise Men's Carol

When the light was born in the carnival sky –
    About the wide world –
The tune was new, the words were wild;
As young as the hills and as old as a Child –
    When the sun came up on the Christmas world.

The dark blew off in the carnival wind –
    About the wide world –
The sea shook tides for all its salt worth
At a snippet of heaven discovered on earth –
    When the sun came up on the Christmas world.

The fields awoke to that carnival day –
    About the wide world –
It was summer in winter and harvest in spring;
Kingcup and kingfisher mobbed their king?
    When the sun came up on the Christmas world.

Spink under shadow and lark in the light –
    About the wide world –
Twanged into song on branch and on wing;
If *you'd* been there you'd have *had* to sing –
    When the sun came up on the Christmas world.

When God was born that High Carnival Morn –
    About the wide world –
When beginning began and the Word was with men,
It was you and I who were young again –
    When the sun came up on the Christmas world.

Congratulations, Herod,
      On a bargain firm and sound,
Two thousand children done to death
      But you're still over-ground.
You've signed your name for future fame,
      Deny your claim, who can –
Congratulations, Herod,
      You're a business man.

You've won honour for your country;
      You've saved the world from war;
You've made a better bargain than
      Man ever made before.
All stress and strife and controversy
      Pinched out in the pod– –
Congratulations, Herod,
      You've done better than God.

Congratulations, Herod –
      But when all is done and said,
The final sums of history
      May add up in the red.
For all speculating business men
      Must learn this market trend:
That the best-seeming bargains
      Cost the most in the end.

Carol for the Watchers

The first night, the first night,
    The night that Christ was born,
His mother looked in His eyes and saw
    Her Maker in her son.

The twelfth night, the twelfth night,
    After Christ was born,
The Wise Men found the Child and knew
    Their search had just begun.

Eleven thousand two hundred and fifty nights,
    After Christ was born,
A dead man hung in the Child's light
    And the sun went down at noon.

Six hundred thousand and thereabouts nights,
    After Christ was born,
    What is now left in the world to see?
I look at you and you look at me,
    And neither knows the sun.

But the last night, the last night,
    Since ever Christ was born,
What His mother saw will be seen again,
And what was found by the Three Wise Men,
And the Sun will rise and so may we,
    On the last morn, on Christmas Morn,
Umpteen hundred and eternity.

A LOCAL HABITATION

(1972)

. . . and gives to airy nothing
A local habitation and a name.
A Midsummer Night's Dream

The Dumb Spirit

Eyes see
The shine and smother
Of world and otherworld –
The dumb spirit
Stifles the breath.

Ears hear
Clamour and song
Flung off the fly-wheel of the straining year –
The dumb spirit
Knots up the tongue.

Hands feel
The braille of creatures'
Meeting and mesh –
The dumb spirit
Dams the flow of the flesh.

Cast out the dumb,
Lord.
Touch ears.
Let spittle un-numb the tongue.
Let there be no impediment on lung or larynx,
And let the breath
Speak plain again.

The Borehole

A huddle of iron jammy-cranes[*]
Straddles the skear,[†] shanks
Rusty from salt rains,
Or halfway up their barnacled flanks
In the flood tide. Paid-up pits
Lounge round the banks,
Turning out red pockets.
The cranking waders stand,
Necks down, bills grinding in their sockets,
Drilling the sand.
A steam-pipe whistles, the clanged iron bells;
Five hundred feet of limestone shudders and
Creaks down all its strata'd spine of ammonites and shells
And a vertical worm of stone is worried
Out from the earth's core.
The daylight falls
Westward with the ebb, before
The night-shift buzzer calls:
But what is it sticks in the bird's gullet –
Rubble or crystal, dross or ore?

[*] Jammy-cranes – herons.
[†] Skear – a bank of shingle or stones exposed at low tide.

The Whisperer

For twenty months I whispered,
    Spoke aloud
    Not one word,
Except when the doctor, checking my chest, said:
    'Say Ninety-nine',
    And, from the mine
Of my throat, hauling up my voice like a load of metal, I
    Said 'Ninety-nine.'
    From sixteen?
years-old to my eighteenth birthday I whispered clock
    And season round;
    Made no sound
More than the wind that entered without knocking
    Through the door
    That wasn't there
Or the slid-wide window that un-shuttered half the wall of my
    Shepherd's bothy
    Of a chalet.
In the hushed sanatorium night I coughed in whispers
    To stray cats
    And dogs that
Stalked in from the forest fogs to the warmth of my anthracite
    stove,
    And at first light
    Of shrill July
To the robin winding its watch beside spread trays of cedars.
    Day after day
    My larynx lay

In dry dock until whispering seemed
        The normal way
        Of speaking: I
Was surprised at the surprise on the face of strangers
        Who wondered why
        I was so shy.
When I talked to next-bed neighbours, out-of-breath on the
        Gravel track,
        They whispered back
As if the practice were infectious. Garrulous as a budgie,
        I filled the air
        Of my square
Thermometered and Lysolled cage with the agitated
        Wheezes, squeaks
        And wind-leaks
Of my punctured Northumbrian pipes. And when the doctor
        asked me
        How I felt, 'I'm
        Feeling fine,'
I whispered – my temperature down to thirty-seven,
        The sore grate
        Soothed from my throat,
And all the winds of Hampshire to ventilate my lungs.

Two winters went whispered away before I ventured
        Out of my cage,
        Over the hedge,
On to the chalky chines, the sparse, pony-trodden, adder-ridden
        Grass. Alone
        Among pine
Trunks I whispered comfortable sermons to
        Congregations
        Of worms. Patients

On exercise in copse or on common, sighting me
           At distance, gave
           Me a wave,
And I in reply blew a blast on my police-
           man's whistle,
           Meaning: 'Listen.
Wait! Come closer. I've something to tell.'
           But when tea?
           time brought me
To drawing-room and chatter, the thunder of shook cups,
           Crack of laughter,
           Stunned and baffled
Me. I bawled in whispers four-inch from the ear
           Of him or her
           Unheeded. Words,
Always unheard, failed even articulate me.
           Frantic, I'd rap
           Table or clap
Hands, crying: 'Listen, for God's sake listen!' And suddenly the
           room
           Fell silent,
           Waiting, and I
Words failing again, fell silent too.
                         The world moved
           Noisily on.
           My larynx soon
Was afloat again but my life still drifts in whispers
           I shout out loud
           To no crowd,
Straining to be heard above its strangling murmur, but
           Look for one face
           Lit with the grace

Of listening, the undeadened brow that marks an undeafened
        Ear. I try
        To catch an eye;
Nod, nudge, wink, beckon, signal with clicked
        Fingers, roll
        Words to a ball
And toss them for the wind to play with. Life roars round me like
        A dynamo.
        I stump, stamp, blow
Whistle over and over, staring into the rowdy air, seeking
        You or you,
        Anyone who
Can lip-read the words of my whisper as clear as the clang of a
        bell,
        Can see me say:
        'Wait! Wait!
        Come closer;
        I've something to tell.'

The Black Guillemot

Midway between Fleswick and St Bees North Head,
The sun in the west,
All Galloway adrift on the horizon;
The sandstone red
As dogwood; sea-pink, sea campion and the sea itself
Flowering in clefts of the cliff –
And down on one shelf,
Dozen on dozen pressed side by side together,
White breast by breast,
Beaks to the rock and tails to the fish-stocked sea,
The guillemots rest

Restlessly. Now and then,
One shifts, clicks free of the cliff,
Wings whirling like an electric fan –
Silhouette dark from above, with underbelly gleaming
White as it banks at the turn –
Dives, scoops, skims the water,
Then, with all Cumberland to go at, homes
To the packed slum again,
The rock iced with droppings.

I swing my binoculars into the veer of the wind,
Sight, now, fifty yards from shore,
That rarer auk: all black,
But for two white patches where the wings join the back,
Alone like an off-course migrant
(Not a bird of his kind
Nesting to the south of him in England),
Yet self-subsistent as an Eskimo,
Taking the huff if so much as a feather
Lets on his pool and blow-hole
In the floating pack-ice of gulls.

But, turn the page of the weather,
Let the moon haul up the tides and the pressure-hose of spray
Swill down the lighthouse lantern – then,
When boats keep warm in harbour and bird-watchers in bed,
When the tumble-home of the North Head's rusty hull
Takes the full heave of the storm,
The hundred white and the one black flock
Back to the same rock.

Boo to a Goose

'You couldn't say Boo to a goose,' my grandmother said
When I skittered howling in from the back street – my head
With a bump the size of a conker from a stick that someone
    threw,
Or my eyes rubbed red
From fists stuffed in to plug the blubbing. 'Not Boo to a goose,'
    she said,
But coddled me in the kitchen, gave me bread
Spread with brown sugar – her forehead,
Beneath a slashed, ash-grey bark of hair,
Puckered in puzzle at this old-fashioned child
Bright enough at eight to read the ears off
His five unlettered uncles, yet afraid
Of every giggling breeze that blew.
'There's nowt to be scared about,' she said,
'A big lad like you!'

But not as big as a goose –
                              or not the geese I knew,
Free-walkers of Slagbank Green.
From morning-lesson bell to supper-time
They claimed lop-sided common-rights between
Tag-ends of sawn-off, two-up-two-down streets
And the creeping screes of slag.
They plucked their acres clean
Of all but barley-grass and mud. Domesticated but never tamed,
They peeked down on you from their high
Spiked periscopes. No dog would sniff within a hundred yards
Of their wing-menaced ground.

At the first sound
Of a bicycle ring they'd tighten ranks,
Necks angled like bayonets, throttles sizzling,
And skein for the bare knees and the cranking shanks.
They were guarded like Crown Jewels. If any man were seen
To point a finger to a feather
He'd end up with boot-leather for his dinner.
They harried girls in dreams – and my lean
Spinning-wheel legs were whittled even thinner
From trundling round the green's extremest hem
To keep wide of their way.
No use daring me to say
Boo to them.

The girls grew up and the streets fell down;
Gravel and green went under the slag; the town
Was eroded into the past. But half a century later
Three geese – two wild, streaked brown-grey-brown
As the bog-cottoned peat, and one white farm-yard fly-off –
Held sentry astride a Shetland lochan. The crumbled granite
Tumbled down brae and voe-side to the tide's
Constricted entry; the red-throated diver jerked its clown?
striped neck, ducked, disappeared and perked up from the water
A fly-cast further on. The three geese took no notice.
But the moment I stepped from the hide of the car
The white one stiffened, swivelled, lowered its trajectory,
And threatened towards me. Then,
Under the outer Arctic's summer arc of blue,
With a quick blink that blacked out fifty years
And a forgotten fear repeating in my stomach,
I found myself staring, level-along and through,
The eyes of that same slagbank braggart
I couldn't say Boo to.

The Elvers

An iron pipe
Syphoning gallons of brine
From the hundred foot below sea-level mine –
A spring salty as mussels,
Bilberry-stained with ore;
And the pink, dry-paper thrift rustles
In the draught made by the spray
As the pumps thrust the water upward
To a rock-locked bay.

And, quick in the brown burn,
Black whips that flick and shake,
Live darning-needles with big-eye heads –
Five-inch elvers
That for twice five seasons snake
Through the earth's turn and return of water
To seep with the swell into rifts of the old workings
And be churned out here on cinder beds and fern.

The pumps pour on.
The elvers shimmy in the weed. And I,
Beneath my parochial complement of sky,
Plot their way
From Sargasso Sea to Cumberland,
From tide to pit,
Knowing the why of it
No more than they.

Bee Orchid at Hodbarrow

A hundred years ago
The swash channel
Filled at high water
And swilled dry
In runnels of sand at low –
Under the lea
Of the limestone shore,
Mine-shaft and funnel,
And the old light-house
On its stack of rejected ore.

Fifty years ago
The new sea-wall
Cordon'd and claimed
A parish no one wanted,
A Jordan Valley without the Jordan,
Neither sea nor land,
Lower than low
Ebb-mark, arid
As wrack left lifted
High on the sand.

Only a backwash
Of rain drained inward
To a sumpy hollow
Above the old drifts –
Subsided tunnels
Open to the sky,
To rabbit and plover

Neither submarine
Nor dry-land level,
Neither under nor over.

But now on the bare
Pate of the ground
See the bee orchid –
Neither plant nor animal,
A metaphysical
Conceit of a flower –
Heading the queue there,
First come, first served,
Where even ragwort's rare.

Decoy queens,
Honeyed and furred,
Linger and cling
To each lolling lobe;
Nervous, green-veined,
Lilac sepals
Prick at the twitch
Of a pollinating wing.

And stiff as a quill
In the splash of the grasses,
The whole articulated
Body of the flower –
Bloom, stem and leaf –
Is tense with need
To breed, to seed,
To colonize the new-found,
New-sunk island,
To snatch the brief

Between-tide hour
Of this limestone summer,
Before the sea
Pours in again
In three or four
Hundred years' time.

Hodbarrow Flooded

Where once the bogies bounced along hummocking tracks,
A new lake spreads its edges.
Where quarried ledges were loaded with red-mould ore,
Old winding towers
Up-ended float on glass.
Where once the shafts struck down through yielding limestone,
Black coot and moorhen
Lay snail-wakes on the water.

At seventy fathom
My Uncle Jack was killed
With half a ton of haematite spilled on his back.
They wound him up to the light
Still gasping for air.

Not even the rats can gasp there now:
For, beneath the greening spoil of a town's life-time,
The sixty, seventy,
Ninety fathom levels
Are long pipes and throttles of unflowing water,
Stifled cavities,
Lungs of a drowned man.

The Riddle

Why is a baby
Like a railway engine? – I
Knew the answer, maybe
Forty years ago:
The night old Rustyknob
Of the jerry-laid iron mine,
All duck-waddle and puff,
Dived like a gannet,
Stream-feathered and slender,
Plumb in the deeps of the mine.
And the sand closed like water
Over piston-rod and spoke
Leaving not even the tender
Behind for a schoolboy's joke.

We stood in the steaming
November air
Staring at rails
Bent to no junction;
And switch-point levers
Left without function
Swivelled eyes wide
Down tracks of drifting shales –
And the son of the day-shift engine driver
Stood by my side.

The sand's slow tide
Flowed in and filled the crater;
Salted sleeper and chair.
Bolt and signal wire
Reddened like raspberries
In the soggy sea-air.
Thrift and sea-holly
Spilled on the dolly-tub rim,
Trefoil and clover
Yellowed it over,
Till not a dip the depth of a saucer
Scored the spot where the night-shift driver
Fought and fell clear,
And the bumpers bored down
To an underground siding,
Hauling a thousand brown
Bogey-loads of ore.

The dune-fly dances
In the jittery sun,
And skewers of marram
Peg down the ground-sheet sand.
But why is a baby? –
I forgot the answer
That muggy November
All Souls' Eve,
The night the engine died,
And only the old remember now,
And only the young believe.

Windscale

The toadstool towers infest the shore:
Stink-horns that propagate and spore
    Wherever the wind blows.
Scafell looks down from the bracken band,
And sees hell in a grain of sand,
    And feels the canker itch between his toes.

This is a land where dirt is clean,
And poison pasture, quick and green,
    And storm sky, bright and bare;
Where sewers flow with milk, and meat
Is carved up for the fire to eat,
    And children suffocate in God's fresh air.

The Elm Decline

The crags crash to the tarn; slow?
motion corrosion of scree.
From scooped corries,
bare as slag,
black sykes ooze
through quarries of broken boulders.
The sump of the tarn
slumps into its mosses – bog
asphodel, sundew, sedges –
a perpetual
sour October
yellowing the moor.

        Seven
thousand years ago
trees grew
high as this tarn. The pikes
were stacks and skerries
spiking the green,
the tidal surge
of oak, birch, elm,
ebbing to ochre
and the wrackwood of backend.

                              Then
round the year Three
Thousand BC,
the proportion of elm pollen
preserved in peat
declined from twenty
per cent to four.

                    Stone axes,
chipped clean from the crag-face,
ripped the hide off the fells.
Spade and plough
scriated the bared flesh,
skewered down to the bone.
The rake flaked into fragments
and kettlehole tarns
were shovelled chock-full
of a rubble of rotting rocks.

                             Today
electric landslips
crack the rock;
drills tunnel it;
valleys go under the tap.
Dynamited runnels
channel a poisoned rain,
and the fractured ledges
are scoured and emery'd
by wind-to-wind rubbings
of nuclear dust.

                    Soon
the pikes, the old
bottlestops of lava,
will stand scraped bare,
nothing but air round stone
and stone in air,
ground-down stumps
of a skeleton jaw –

                    Until
under the scree,
under the riddled rake,
beside the outflow of the reedless lake,
no human eye remains to see
a landscape man
helped nature make.

Scree

A million centuries it grew like a great tree
   Under the sea,
The wrack-ringed rock, lifting its branches higher
   Than the fire
Of black volcanoes burning in the green water. Coal
   Sprang from its bole
Like a parasitic plant; surf and sand
   Salted and
Silted it. Yet still the blunt trunk thrust
   Out through the crust
Shedding the paleozoic years like bark,
   While habitual, dark
Roots hankered back to unfossiliferous blocks
   Of rocks that made the rocks.
The wind rips off the wrap of sand till the tree stands bare
   In the hacksawing air,
Or under the rub of water, seep and sump,
   Worn to a stump,
Flakes away rind in a mildew of mist.
   Green-winged frost
With a woodpecker's prod and point
   Gimlets each joint;
Witch's broom, oak-apple, fungus, gall,
   Canker all
The crackles of the cork. A drool
   Of wood-rot and toadstool
Oozes from crevices, squirrel-and mouse?
   hole and tom-tit's house
Down to the ant-hill roots.

                        The tree
            Disintegrates.

                        Scree
        Is the autumn fall of the deciduous rock;
                    Acorn-grey Oc-
        tober of stone; compost of loam and lime;
                    Cold leaf-mould of time.
        Prolific as bacteria the one-cell seconds breed,
                    Corrupting wall and weed,
                        Depositing new seed.

September on the Mosses

Wait, tide, wait;
Let the mosses slide
In runnels and counter-flow of rock-pool green,
Where web-foot mud-weeds preen
Leaves spread in the sunshine; where
On slow air-ripples the marsh aster lays
Innocuous snare of sea-anemone rays.

Wait, tide, wait;
Behind your wide?
as-winter ebb the poplars of the waves
Turn up their underleaves of grey.
Thunder-blue shadows boom across the bay.
But here the silt is green, the salt is bright,
And every grass-tongue licks its summerful of light.

Autumnal tide,
Mauve as Michaelmas daisies, bide
Our while and summer's. Let the viscous sun
Percolate the turf. Let small becks run
Yellow for ever with shine, and the floor of this moment
Hold back time and shut the gate.
Wait, tide, wait.

Deciduous tide,
On the willow whips of inshore billows the inside
Edge is brown. Crying 'Never!'
Canutes no due tomorrow,
And now is ever
By being not by lasting. So
With pride let this long-as-life hour go,
And flow, tide, flow.

One Minute

To my Wife

Fifteen years ago –
The shut-down dark
Of hibernating February.
The park
Trees, ghosted in an underglow
Of lamp-wash, straining
Upwards to blackness;
Not even a star
To demonstrate by not being seen
The shape of the church-tower.
But spilled
On the far
Cruck of the hill
The red-green rakings
Of the coke smoulder of day –
'Look!' you said,
Pointing to March,
The un-cocooning of a new year.

Fifteen more, and spring
Again unwinds itself;
Birds shout
In the thickening dusk.
The church-tower sprouts a pale
Blue steeple under the new moon;
The wickered willows
Still trellis the west;
Safe in the glowing graveyard

[290]

Another generation is put to bed.
One minute tells the tale.
And yet to make
Count of, find words for, all
These fifteen
Years add up to, mean
And span
('Yes!' you said,
Pointing to the small
Re-kindling of the dead end of day)
Could hardly take
That minute less than
Fifteen years.

An Absence of Islands

Look west
from Cumberland,
east from the North Sea shore,
where the wind is a spume of tossed terns and fulmars
of fumes with smothering feathers of soot;
look beyond seaweed and seawage,
pebbles and quck-sand and the oiled ebb channel –
and always,
at the far rim of the sea's grooved disk,
whatever the direction, whatever the slide of tide,
in an absence of islands
the horizon seems the same.

The Tune the Old Cow Died of

'The tune the old cow died of,'
My grandmother used to say
When my uncle played the flute.
She hadn't seen a cow for many a day,
Shut in by slate
Walls that bound her
To scullery and yard and soot?
blackened flowerpots and hart's-tongue fern.
She watched her fourteen sons grow up around her
In a back street,
Blocked at one end by crags of slag,
Barred at the other by the railway goods-yard gate.
The toot of the flute
Piped to a parish where never cow could earn
Her keep – acres of brick
With telegraph poles and chimneys reared up thick
As ricks in a harvest field.
My grandmother remembered
Another landscape where the cattle
Waded halfway to the knees
In swish of buttercup and yellow rattle,
And un-shorn, parasite-tormented sheep
Flopped down like grey bolsters in the shade of trees,
And the only sound
Was the whine of a hound
In the out-of-hunting-season summer,
Or the cheep of wide-beaked, new-hatched starlings,
Or the humdrum hum of the bees.

Then

A cow meant milk, meant cheese, meant money,
And when a cow died
With foot-and-mouth or wandered out on the marshes
And drowned at the high tide,
The children went without whatever their father had promised
When she was a girl
There was nothing funny,
My grandmother said,
About the death of a cow,
And it isn't funny now
To millions hungrier even than she was then.
So when the babies cried,
One after each for over fourteen years,
Or the flute squeaked at her ears,
Or the council fire-alarm let off a scream
Like steam out of a kettle and the whole mad town
Seemed fit to blow its lid off – she could find
No words to ease her mind
Like those remembered from her childhood fears:
'The tune the old cow died of.'

Have You Been to London?

'Have you been to London?'
My grandmother asked me.
                                    'No.' –
China dogs on the mantelshelf.
Paper blinds at the window,
Three generations simmering on the bright black lead,
And the kettle filled to the neb,
Spilled over long ago.

I blew into the room, threw
My scholarship cap on the rack;
Wafted visitors up the flue
With the draught of my coming in –
Ready for Saturday's mint imperials,
Ready to read
The serial in *Titbits*, the evangelical
Tale in the parish magazine,
Under the green
Glare of the gas,
Under the stare of my grandmother's Queen.

My grandmother burnished her sleek steel hair –
Not a tooth in her jaw
Nor alphabet in her head,
Her spectacles lost before I was born,
Her lame leg stiff in the sofa corner,
Her wooden crutch at the steady:
'They shut doors after them
In London,' she said.

I crossed the hearth and thumped the door *to*;
Then turned to Saturday's stint,
My virtuosity of print
And grandmother's wonder:
Reading of throttler and curate,
Blood, hallelujahs and thunder,
While the generations boiled down to one
And the kettle burned dry
In a soon grandmotherless room;

Reading for forty years,
Till the print swirled out like a down-catch of soot
And the wind howled round
A world left cold and draughty,
Un-latched, un-done,
By all the little literate boys
Who hadn't been to London.

On the Closing of Millom Ironworks

September 1968

Wandering by the heave of the town park, wondering
Which way the day will drift,
On the spur of a habit I turn to the feathered
Weathercock of the furnace chimneys.
                                        But no grey smoke-tail
Pointers the mood of the wind. The hum
And blare that for a hundred years
Drummed at the town's deaf ears
Now fills the air with the roar of its silence.
They'll need no more to swill the slag-dust off the windows;
The curtains will be cleaner
And the grass plots greener
Round the Old Folk's council flats.
The tanged autumnal mist
Is filtered free of soot and sulphur,
And the wind blows in untainted.
It's beautiful to breathe the sharp night air.
But, morning after morning, there
They stand, by the churchyard gate,
Hands in pockets, shoulders to the slag,
The men whose fathers stood there back in '28,
When their sons were at school with me.
                                        The town
Rolls round the century's bleak orbit.
                              Down
On the ebb-tide sands, the five-funnelled
Battleship of the furnace lies beached and rusting;
Run aground, not foundered;
Not a crack in her hull;

Lacking but a loan to float her off.

                                  The Market
Square is busy as the men file by
To sign on at the 'Brew'.* But not a face
Tilts upward, no one enquires of the sky.
The smoke prognosticates no how
Or why of any practical tomorrow.
For what does it matter if it rains all day?
And what's the good of knowing
Which way the wind is blowing
When whichever way it blows it's a cold wind now.

* The local term for 'Bureau' – i.e. Labour Exchange – widely used in the '30s.

Nicholson, Suddenly

From the Barrow Evening Mail, *Thurs, 13th Feb.,*1969.

'NICHOLSON—(Suddenly) on February 11, Norman,
aged 57 years, beloved husband of Mona Nicholson,
and dear father of Gerald, of 6 Atkinson Street, Haverigg,
Millom.'

So Norman Nicholson is dead!
I saw him just three weeks ago
Standing outside a chemist's shop,
His smile alight, his cheeks aglow.
I'd never seen him looking finer:
'I can't complain at all,' he said,
'But for a touch of the old angina.'
Then hobbled in for his prescription.
Born in one town, we'd made our start,
Though not in any way related,
Two years and three streets apart,
Under one nominal description:
'Nicholson, Norman', entered, dated,
In registers of birth and school.
In 1925 we sat
At the same desk in the same class –
Me, chatty, natty, nervous, thin,
Quick for the turn of the teacher's chin;
Silent, shy and smiling, he,
And fleshed enough for two of me –
An unidentical near twin
Who never pushed his presence in
When he could keep it out.

For seven
Years after that each neither knew,
Nor cared much, where or even whether
The other lived. And then, together,
We nearly booked out berths to heaven: –
Like a church weathercock, *I* crew
A graveyard cough and went to bed
For fifteen months; *he* dropped a lead
Pipe on his foot and broke them both.
They wheeled him home to his young wife
Half-cripped for the rest of life.

In three decades or more since then
We met, perhaps, two years in ten
In shops or waiting for a bus;
Greeted each other without fuss,
Just: 'How do, Norman?' – Didn't matter
Which of us spoke – we said the same.
And now and then we'd stop to natter:
'How's the leg?' or 'How's the chest?' –
He a crock below the waist
And me a crock above it.
Blessed
Both with a certain home-bred gumption,
We stumped our way across the cobbles
Of half a lifetime's bumps and roughness –
He short in step and me in wind,
Yet with a kind of wiry toughness.
Each rather sorry for the other,
We chose the road that suited best –
Neither inscribed the sky with flame;
Neither disgraced the other's name.

And now, perhaps, one day a year
The town will seem for half a minute
A place with one less person in it,
When I remember I'll not meet
My unlike double in the street.
Postmen will mix us up no more,
Taking my letters to his door,
For which I ought to raise a cheer.
But can I stir myself to thank
My lucky stars, when there's a blank
Where his stars were? For I'm left here,
Wearing his name as well as mine,
Finding the new one doesn't fit,
And, though I'll make the best of it,
Sad that such things had to be –
But glad, still, that it wasn't me.

Old Man at a Cricket Match

'It's mending worse,' he said,
Bending west his head,
Strands of anxiety ravelled like old rope,
Skitter of rain on the scorer's shed
His only hope.

Seven down for forty-five,
Catches like stings from a hive,
And every man on the boundary appealing –
An evening when it's bad to be alive,
And the swifts squealing.

Yet without boo or curse
He waits leg-break or hearse,
Obedient in each to law and letter –
Life and the weather mending worse,
Or worsening better.

A Local Preacher's Goodbye

'I'll meet you again up there' –
He pointed to the smoke
With black umbrella finger
(The chimneys tall as hymns,
Fuming with extemporary prayer) –
'I'll see you all up there,'
                    He said.

Six boys or seven
In the dark October drizzle,
Class tickets in our pockets,
Ready to leave Heaven
Locked in with the hymn-books;
Supper and bed
Hard on by the Market Clock –
'Good night, Mr Fawcett, sir,'
                    We said.

Forty years of soot and rain;
a Bible-insured
Ghost of chapel steward
And manufacturer of aerated waters,
With grey-ginger beard
Bubbling my unwritten poetry –
'Grand seeing you again!',
                    I say.

Bond Street

'Bond Street,' I said, 'Now where the devil's that?' –
The name of one whose face has been forgotten. –
He watched me from a proud-as-Preston hat;
His briefcase fat with business. 'See, it's written
First on my list. Don't you know your own town?' –
'Bond Street?' – Turning it over like an old coin,
Thumbing it, testing for signs. – 'I copied it down
From a map in the Reading Room. In the mean-
time, I've a policy here...' – Yes, on a *map*
Bond Street once looked the first of streets, more
Rakish than the Prince of Wales, the peak of the cap
Jaunted at then ungathered orchards of ore,
Damsons of haematite. Yet not a house
Was built there and the road remained unmade,
For there was none to pay the rates – a mouse
And whippet thoroughfare, engineered in mud,
Flagged with the green-slab leaves of dock and plantain,
A free run for the milk cart to turn round
From either of the two back-alleys shunted
End-on against it. But the birds soon found
Sites where the Council couldn't. From last year's broccoli
    and old
Brass bedsteads joggled in to make a fence,
Among the pigeon lofts and hen-huts, in the cold
Green-as-a-goosegog twilight, the throstles sense
That here is the one street in all the town
That no one ever died in, that never failed
Its name or promise. The iron dust blows brown.
I turned to my enquirer. – 'Bond Street I know well.

'You'll sell no insurance there.' – 'I could insure
'The deaf and dumb,' he replied, 'against careless talk.' –
'Whatever you choose,' I said. 'A mile past the Square,
'Then ask again. Hope you enjoy your walk.'

To the Memory of a Millom Musician

Harry Pelleymounter,
Day by half-pay day,
Served saucepans, fire-lighters, linseed oil
Over his father's counter;
But hard on shutting-up time
He snapped the yale and stayed
Alone with the rolled linoleum
And made the shop-dusk twang.

Harry played
Saxophone, piano,
Piano-accordion
At Christmas party and Saturday hop,
While we in the after-homework dark
Rang smut-bells, sang
'Yes, yes, YES, we have no',
And clicked ink-smitted fingers
At a down-at-heel decade.

The crumbling thirties
Were fumbled and riddled away;
Dirty ten bob coupons
Dropped from the pockets of war.
And Harry, dumped in the lateral
Moraine of middle age,
Strummed back the golden dole-days
When the boys with never a chance
Went without dinner
For a tanner for the dance.

Now Harry's daughter,
Fatherless at fifteen,
Is knitting a history thesis
Of Millom in between
Her youth and Harry's: –
Statistics of gas and water
Rates, percentage of unemployed,
Standard of health enjoyed
By the bare-foot children the police ran dances
To buy boots for – and Harry played.

Pulling at threads of the dead years,
The minutes taken as read –
Spectacled, earnest, unaware
That what the Chairman left unsaid,
The print in the dried-up throat, the true
Breath of the paper bones, once blew
Through Harry's soft-hummed, tumbled tunes
She never listened to.

Great Day

'I gave him an – *err*,' my father said, meaning
Masonic handshake: holding his fingers
As if they still were sticky from the royal touch.
And I, at an upstairs window (the afternoon
Raining down on the Square, the Holborn Hill Brass
   Bandsmen
Blowing the water out of their tubas) watched
His Royal Highness conducted through the puddles
To my father's brotherly clasp.
                     Out in the wet,
Beside the broken billboards and the derelict joiner's yard,
Two hundred primary scholars soaked and cheered,
Unseeing and unseen.
                  At five o'clock that morning
We'd climbed the Jubilee Hill in the drizzling forelight
To view, in ninety-nine per cent eclipse, a sun
That never rose at all. The smoke from early fires
Seeped inconspicuously into the mist; the 5.30
Ironworks buzzer boomed out like a fog-horn. Click,
On the nick of the clock, the calculated dawn
Shied back on itself, birds knocked off shouting,
And the light went home to roost. Two minutes later
The twist of the globe turned up the dimmer
And day began again to try to begin.
                    It rained,
On and off, for eleven hours, but I
Dry in my window-seat, the sun still in eclipse,
Squinted at the prince through candle-kippered glasses,
Too young to be disappointed, too old to cheer –

Universe and dynasty poised on the tip of one parish –
Eager at last, for *God Save the King* and tea
And my father's now royally contagious hand.

The Cock's Nest

The spring my father died – it was winter, really,
February fill-grave, but March was in
Before we felt the bruise of it and knew
How empty the rooms were that spring
A wren flew to our yard, over Walter Willson's
Warehouse roof and the girls' school playground
From the old allotments that are now no more than a compost
For raising dockens and cats. It found a niche
Tucked behind the pipe of the bathroom outflow,
Caged in a wickerwork of creeper; then
Began to build:
Three times a minute, hour after hour,
Backward and forward to the backyard wall,
Nipping off neb-fulls of the soot-spored moss
Rooted between the bricks. In a few days
The nest was finished. They say the cock
Leases an option of sites and leaves the hen
To choose which nest she will. She didn't choose our yard.
And as March gambolled out, the fat King-Alfred sun
Blared down too early from its tinny trumpet
On new-dug potato-beds, the still bare creeper,
The cock's nest with never an egg in,
And my father dead.

The Seventeenth of the Name

When my grandmother in a carrier's cart, fording the mile and
        a half wide
Ebb of the Duddon, saw the black marsh sprouting
         Furnace and shack,
         'Turn the horse back!'
She cried, but the tide had turned and the horse went on. My
        land-bred grand-
father, harnessed farm hacks to works waggons, shifted grit
         from the quarries,
         And laid down
         The road to the town
Before the town was there. My Uncle Bill,
Bundled in with the eggs and the luggage at fifteen months,
         hatched out to be a blacksmith,
         Served his hour
         To horseless horse-power,
Forged shoes for machines and iron pokers, hooked
Like a butcher's skewer, for my grandmother's kitchen range.

         My Uncle Jack
         Played full back
For the Northern Union and went in second wicket for the
         First Eleven.
One August Monday he smacked a six clean into an excursion
         train –
         'Hit it from here
         To Windermere,'
My grandmother said. He broke his spine down the mine and
         died below ground

(The family's prided loss on the iron front),
　　　　　Left, 'Not to Mourn',
　　　　　A daughter, born
After he died, and a widow who held to his memory fifty years.
My Uncle Tom was a cobbler: under a crack willow of leather
　　　　　shavings
　　　　　Tacked boot, nailed clog,
　　　　　By the twitch of dog?
eared Co-operative gas-jets in the dark of the shoe shop where
My Uncle Jim was manager. He, best-loved uncle
　　　　　And my father's friend,
　　　　　In the end
Out-lived the lot: octogenarian, in a high, stiff collar, he
　　　　　walked his silver-
banded cane down the half-day closings
　　　　　Of a vast, life-lasting,
　　　　　Somnambulist past.
My Uncle George married Jim's wife's sister and left with my
　　　　　Uncle Fred
To be bosses' weighman and men's check-weighman in the
　　　　　same Durham pit. Each
　　　　　Bargained each black
　　　　　Over half tons of slack,
And they went for a walk together every Sunday morning.
My Uncle Bob, a Tom-Thumb tailor, as my grandmother told
　　　　　me,
　　　　　Sat cross-legged all day
　　　　　On a thimble; went to stay
With George, drove out on a motor-bike and rode back in a
　　　　　hearse.
Arnold, the youngest, hung wallpaper; Harry was a waiter;
　　　　　Richard took fits. Three
　　　　　Died in infancy,

Un-christened and un-sistered. One other brother
Left me what an uncle couldn't: – a face, a place, a root
            That drives down deep
            As St George's steeple
Heaves up high. – The church was built in the year that he was
            born. –
The name is painted out on the sun-blind of my father's shop,
            But yellows yet
            In files of *The Millom Gazette*,
And in minutes of the Musical Festival and the Chamber of
            Trade,
And in lead letters on headstones by St George's mound
            It now spells out
            Its what-are-you-going-to-do-about-it
Memorandum. As once when a boy I see it scratched
On backstreet slates and schoolyard gates. Step on the gravel
            and the stones squeak out
            'Nicholson, Nicholson.'
            Whereupon
Grandmother, grandfather, father, seven known
And six clocked-out-before-me uncles stare
            From their chimneyed heaven
            On the seventeenth
Of the name, wondering through the holy smother where the
            family's got to.
And I, in their great-grand-childless streets, rake up for my
            reply
            Damn all but hem
            And haw about them.

SEA TO THE WEST

(1981)

A poet's hope: to be,
like some valley cheese,
local, but prized elsewhere
W. H. Auden, *Epistle to a Godson*

Scafell Pike

Look
Along the well
Of the street,
Between the gasworks and the neat
Sparrow-stepped gable
Of the Catholic chapel,
High
Above tilt and crook
Of the tumbledown
Roofs of the town –
Scafell Pike,
The tallest hill in England.

How small it seems,
So far away,
No more than a notch
On the plate-glass window of the sky!
Watch
A puff of kitchen smoke
Block out peak and pinnacle –
Rock-pie of volcanic lava
Half a mile thick
Scotched out
At the click of an eye.

Look again
In five hundred, a thousand or ten
Thousand years:
A ruin where
The chapel was; brown
Rubble and scrub and cinders where
The gasworks used to be;
No roofs, no town,
Maybe no men;
But yonder where a lather-rinse of cloud pours down
The spiked wall of the sky-line, see,
Scafell Pike
Still there.

Beck

Not the beck only,
Not just the water –
The stones flow also,
Slow
As continental drift,
As the growth of coral,
As the climb
Of a stalagmite.
Motionless to the eye,
Wide cataracts of rock
Pour off the fellside,
Throw up a spume
Of gravel and scree
To eddy and sink
In the blink of a lifetime.
The water abrades,
Erodes; dissolves
Limestones and chlorides;
Organizes its haulage –
Every drop loaded
With a millionth of a milligramme of fell.
The falling water
Hangs steady as stone;
But the solid rock
Is a whirlpool of commotion,
As the fluid strata
Crest the curl of time,
And top-heavy boulders
Tip over headlong,

An inch in a thousand years.
A Niagara of chock-stones,
Bucketing from the crags,
Spouts down the gullies.
Slate and sandstone
Flake and deliquesce,
And in a grey
Alluvial sweat
Ingleborough and Helvellyn
Waste daily away.
The pith of the pikes
Oozes to the marshes,
Slides along the sykes,
Trickles through ditch and dub,
Enters the endless
Chain of water,
The pull of earth's centre –
An irresistible momentum,
Never to be reversed,
Never to be halted,
Till the tallest fell
Runs level with the lowland,
And scree lies flat as shingle,
And every valley is exalted,
Every mountain and hill
Flows slow.

Wall

The wall walks the fell –
Grey millipede on slow
Stone hooves;
Its slack back hollowed
At gulleys and grooves,
Or shouldering over
Old boulders
Too big to be rolled away.
Fallen fragments
Of the high crags
Crawl in the walk of the wall.

A dry-stone wall
Is a wall and a wall,
Leaning together
(Cumberland-and-Westmorland
Champion wrestlers),
Greening and weathering,
Flank by flank,
With filling of rubble
Between the two –
A double-rank
Stone dyke:
Flags and through-
stones jutting out sideways,
Like the steps of a stile.

A wall walks slowly.
At each give of the ground,
Each creak of the rock's ribs,
It puts its foot gingerly,
Arches its hog-holes,
Lets cobble and knee-joint
Settle and grip.
As the slipping fellside
Erodes and drifts,
The wall shifts with it,
Is always on the move.

They built a wall slowly,
A day a week;
Built it to stand,
But not stand still.
They built a wall to walk.

Cloud on Black Combe

The air clarifies. Rain
Has clocked off for the day.

The wind scolds in from Sligo,
Ripping the calico-grey from a pale sky.
Black Combe holds tight
To its tuft of cloud, but over the three-legged island
All the west is shining.

An hour goes by,
And now the starched collars of the eastern pikes
Streak up into a rinse of blue. Every
Inland fell is glinting;
Black Combe alone still hides
Its bald, bleak forehead, balaclava'd out of sight.

Slick fingers of wind
Tease and fidget at wool-end and wisp,
Picking the mist to bits.
Strings and whiskers
Fray off from the cleft hill's
Bilberried brow, disintegrate, dissolve
Into blue liquidity –
Only a matter of time
Before the white is wholly worried away
And Black Combe starts to earn its name again.

But where, in the west, a tide
Of moist and clear-as-a-vacuum air is piling
High on the corried slopes, a light
Fret and haar of hazy whiteness
Sweats off the cold rock; in a cloudless sky
A cloud emulsifies,
Junkets on sill and dyke.
Wool-end and wisp materialize
Like ectoplasm, are twined
And crocheted to an off-white,
Over-the-lughole hug-me-tight;
And Black Combe's ram's-head, butting at the bright
Turfed and brackeny brine,
Gathers its own wool, plucks shadow out of shine.

What the wind blows away
The wind blows back again.

The Shadow of Black Combe

In wise, proverbial days they used to say
That everybody born
Under the shadow of Black Combe
Will come back there to die.

                    Come
Back Arthur, come back Andy, come back Will.
Come home,
While there's still time.

And all you who were shot in France,
Drowned in the Great Lakes,
All exiles and dole-day migrants,
Who swallowed influenza, took TB like snuff –
Get ready to come back. Once
Is not enough.
Get ready to die again.

There's room for you
Under that sprawled, green burial mound,
Under the round,

Turfed, cobble-dashed dome,
Herring-bone masonry of slivered stone,
Where a crag-fenced, shovelled-away entrance
Gill cracks back
To some before-man-made cavern, some
Ordovician catacomb –
For you,
For all the thousand millions of the earth,
Black Combe has room.

But as for me,
I'm staying here,
Not leaving it to chance –
One death will do for me.

Black Combe White

Sixty-mile drive to a reading – arriving by dark,
The audience sparse, the room unsuitable,
And bed in a cold hotel. At 8 a.m.
I draw the curtains, and there, beyond the roof-tops,
Bulging from the flat ledge of the horizon
Like a blister on the white paint of a window-sill,
Black Combe – its unmistakable cleft forehead,
No bigger than a thimble now, outlined in chalk
On the blue distemper of the sky. I turn from the cold
To a room grown more welcoming than before:
'It's been snowing at home!' I say.

                                    Sixty mile back,
Edging the ooze of the estuary mosses – sheep
One side on fire from the level sun; hedges
Clinkering ginger; every dyke and mole-hill
Casting an acre of shadow. And soon
From each rise in the road, each break in the hills' barrier,
Comes glimpse after glimpse of the nearing Combe, first white,
Then patchy, and then streaked white on black,
Darkening and sharpening every minute and every mile.
Home at last to the known tight streets,
The hunched chapels, the long canals of smoke –

And now, from my own doorway, between gable and chimney,
That harsh, scarred brow, entirely stripped of snow,
Impending over yard and attic sky-light,
A dark, parental presence. And when the neighbours tell me:
'The Combe was white last night!' – I don't believe them.
It's always black from here.

Clouded Hills

Though you can't see them,
You know that they are there.

Beneath the Herdwick fleece of mist,
You can feel the heave of the hill.

You can sense the tremor of old volcanoes,
Tense with damped-down fire.

Under a white meringue of cumulus,
Or behind the grey rain-break of a winter's day,

You are aware of the pikes straining high above you,
Spiking up to an unseen sky.

Shingle

It surges down –
Slow underpull
Of heavy grey waves,
Meeting the sea's
Surge upwards.

Never a backflow, always
This crawl of a fall.
On the line of the swell
Each long crest crumbles
Into a sud of stone
Medallions and ovals,
Smooth as butterbeans;
But the shoulder of the wave
Is cumbered with cobbles
The size a stone-waller
Might pile into a barn.

At the bank's bottom step
The obtuse-angled
Thrust of the tide
Shovels the pebbles
Inwards and slant-wise,
For the surf to suck back again
The breadth of a winkle-shell
From where they were before.

A mounded migration
Of crab-backed stones,
Tide by tide, moves
Sideways along the shore.

But here at the highest
Rung of the rise –
A gull's stride under
The shivering overhang
Of sea-spurge and marram –
Only the wildest
Tides arrive
To dump sacks of boulders
On the shrivelled wrack,
Where the stones reside
A while on their circuit,
Inch by inch
Rolling round England.

Dunes

The waves of the sea
Flood up the staggered shore,
Pour along fanned-in runnels,
Slap splashily on flabby jetties;
At the prod of the equinox
They clamber over parapets, wriggle under garden gates,
Scrabble among fuchsias and pebbles,
Batter at sand-bagged doorways,
Savage buckets and brushes and a child's forgotten shoe;
With a frothing of bladderwrack
They bluster and topple
And ebb back to the strand.
The waves of sand
Flood, swell, impend,
And do not ebb at all.

The dunes stalk the town,
Month by month stretching an extra ripple,
A brown reinforcing roll.
They are shovelling the warrens out of the front street;
They are sweeping the foreshore from the window-sills.
Backyard elders and shed and allotment fences
Stand swamped to the knees in the dry silicic flood,
And litter-bins lie buried to the collar.

Away on the hawes the turf rebukes the dunes.
The waves of sand subside, the yellow swell
Calms to a green trough.
Rest-harrow, bedstraw and the wiry dyer's greenweed
Fit a wickered raft of raffia
Along the trapped tide – the moon's pull
Can magnet scarcely a grain above mean sand level.
In the neap of the day the natterjack toad
Occupies an urgent, emergent terrain
Of slithery hillocks and furrows and finger nail screes.
The spiked marram's springy knitting-needles
Purl and entangle what concrete cannot conquer
And the green holds back the brown.

Plant, then, the green, plant marram, plant buckthorn;
Let sea-holly not be uprooted;
Entrench the town behind a fortified zone of grass.

For landward from the horizon the waves of the sea
Flood and ebb,
Flood and ebb,
But here on the verge of the surge the waves of sand
Flood, swell,
Poise themselves, and,
For a little while,
Stay still.

Tide Out

Ebb-tide at sunset:
                    the last light
Slides up the channel
                    as the sea slides down.
Shadows tunnel
                    level into an elevated
Atlantis of sand.
                    The day's green aftermath
Seeps along ginnel
                    and dried-up canal.
Sahara on Sahara,
                    brown ripples of dune
Recede in metallic
                    low relief,
And glimmering, salty
                    teaspoon oases
Simmer and mirage
                    in the frothing dusk.
The filter-feeders
                    burrow back into the mud;
Mussel and barnacle
                    bar their trap-doors.
Walnut-shell worm-casts
                    lean east into umbra,
And the Poor Man's Weather-glass*
                    accepts its hour of air.

---

* Poor Man's Weather-glass: *Laminaria saccharina*,
one of the brown sea weeds or kelps.

Here in the wide
          inter-tidal lull
The estuary suffers
          a Pleistocene age of change.
A night's storm
          recontours a continent;
Sand-slide and canyon
          dissect the exposed plateau.
The tide returns
          to a never-before-visited
Up-thrust and eroded world,
          arid as mica –
World of the wind's shaping and dead
          sand-grain avalanche –
Till, prompt on the tick
          of moon-clock time,
The oxygenated brine
          drowns it back into life.

Plankton

The great un-living energies
Tug at the earth's
Fluid overcoat,
Shake it like a blanket.
The moon applies brakes
And the volts spark off.
The battering wet
Battery of waves
Flashes sheet lightning
And the tides thunder
Under a ninety-
Million-mile-off sun.

But inches below
The enveloping film
Between brine and vapour,
The lesser energies
Explode into self-propulsion
Single cells
Developing fins,
Tentacles, tails;
A tiny octopus,
Rayed like the sun,
That moves as the sun can't.

The earth turns its neck
And the sun exits;
And, dead on the dark,
The sea's cuticle
Phosphoresces with life,
Glows with the fry
And minutiae
That build up the body of the whale.

Dawn
Hatches out a spawn of glitter.
A bacterium
Becomes aware of itself,
Hears its own echo.
As the white day
Climbs up the sky,
The lesser energies,
From a billion billion
Microscopic eyes,
Look back at a blind sun.

Sea to the West

When the sea's to the west
The evenings are one dazzle –
You can find no sign of water.
Sun upflows the horizon;
Waves of shine
Heave, crest, fracture,
Explode on the shore;
The wide day burns
In the incandescent mantle of the air.

Once, fifteen,
I would lean on handlebars,
Staring into the flare,
Blinded by looking,
Letting the gutterings and sykes of light
Flood into my skull.

Then, on the stroke of bedtime,
I'd turn to the town,
Cycle past purpling dykes
To a brown drizzle
Where black-scum shadows
Stagnated between backyard walls.
I pulled the warm dark over my head
Like an eiderdown.

Yet in that final stare when I
(Five times, perhaps, fifteen)
Creak protesting away –
The sea to the west,
The land darkening –
Let my eyes at the last be blinded
Not by the dark
But by dazzle.

Weeds

Some people are flower lovers.
I'm a weed lover.

Weeds don't need planting in well-drained soil;
They don't ask for fertilizer or bits of rag to scare away birds.
They come without invitation;
And they don't take the hint when you want them to go.
Weeds are nobody's guests:
More like squatters.

Coltsfoot laying claim to every new-dug clump of clay;
Pearlwort scraping up a living between bricks from a ha'porth of
    mortar;
Dandelions you daren't pick or you know what will happen;
Sour docks that make a first-rate poultice for nettle-stings;
And flat-foot plantain in the back street, gathering more dust
    than the dustmen.

Even the names are a folk-song:
Fat hen, rat's tail, cat's ear, old men's baccy and Stinking Billy
Ring a prettier chime for me than honeysuckle or jasmine,
And Sweet Cicely smells cleaner than Sweet William though she's
    barred from the garden.

And they have their uses, weeds.
Think of the old, worked-out mines:
Quarries and tunnels, earth scorched and scruffy, torn-up
    railways, splintered sleepers,
And a whole Sahara of grit and smother and cinders.

But go in summer and where is all the clutter?
For a new town has risen of a thousand towers,
Every spiky belfry humming with a peal of bees.
Rosebay willow-herb:
Only a weed!

Flowers are for wrapping in cellophane to present as a bouquet;
Flowers are for prize arrangements in vases and silver tea-pots;
Flowers are for plaiting into funeral wreaths.
You can keep your flowers.
Give me weeds.

Toadstools

October is springtime
For mushrooms and toadstools,
For mole-hill rings
Of Parasol, Snow Bonnet,
Ink Cap and Death Cap,
Beef-steak and burnt-out
King Alfred Cakes.
You may not care a rap
What name each takes,
But eat the wrong one
And you'll soon know you've done it.
Flitters and off-comes
Of ground-damps and dews;
Chlorophyll-lackers,
Slackers and shirkers,
Puff-lumps with no green
Blood in their veins;
Plants that toil not,
That never learn to
Earn their daily
Crumbs of sun;
White octopus-threads,
Under bark, under soil,
That suck dear death
Out of petal and frond,
With never a summering,
Never a giving
Of pollen or seed –
But a parasite-toll

On the whole green set-up.
There are more species
Of moulds and fungi
Than of all the flowering
Plants of the earth –
And the flowers, under lowering
Back-end skies,
Dying, admit:
It's one way of living.

Haytiming

'It's late so soon,' he said –
The sun still high but the day nearly over,
The weed at July and summer toppling.
Away in the intake,
The scaled-out grass sprawled sodden, the ewes wanted clipping,
And the lambs were as big as their mothers.
He stared across the dale.
On its eastern shoulder every cobble and clint
Was seven-times magnified under the lens of light;
The other slope was plunged in a reservoir of shadow.
Bracken, rank and viscous, stank like compost,
The rowans were already reddening,
And the rag-mat of autumn lay coiled up in the corries,
Waiting to be rolled out over fell-foot and byre.
He pushed segged thumbs through hair too early grey,
And said again: 'That's the trouble with summer –
It's late so soon.'

Nobbut God

First on, there was nobbut God.
Genesis, I, v. I., *Yorkshire Dialect Translation.*

First on
There was silence.
And God said:
'Let there be clatter.'

The wind, unclenching,
Runs its thumbs
Along dry bristles of Yorkshire Fog.

The mountain ousel
Oboes its one note.

After rain
Water lobelia
Drips like a tap
On the tarn's tight surface-tension.

But louder,
And every second nearer,
Like chain explosions
From furthest nebulae
Light-yearing across space:
The thudding of my own blood.

'It's nobbut me,'
Says God.

The Cathedral

They built the great cathedrals
By laying stone on stone:
They built *this* one
By taking stone away.

Take away the grey
Weathered outcrop, the glint of crystal,
Black heather and yellow pepper
And rowan, up its lithe hose-pipe
Gushing green into blue;
Take away the fell walls,
Slate-slab roofings, tile-hung frontages,
And the worn flagstones of a farm kitchen;
Take away the rock and all that comes out of the rock –
And what you're left with
Is this hollow quarry
We call 'The Cathedral'.

Said the old philosophers
Of the Negative Way:
There is no road to God
Through the landscape of man's imaginings.

Forget
All you've ever thought of;
Forget rock and sky;
All human mediation
Of finger, lip and eye;
Objects, ideas of objects,

Ideas of ideas;
Forget everything that God is not –
And what you're left with
Will be no further from what God is
Than this hollow quarry
Is from the built splendour
We call a cathedral.

'The Cathedral' is the name given to a huge cavern in an abandoned
slate quarry near Little Langdale in Cumbria.

Fjord

This ice-scoop, this
Sunk valley,
Drowned inwards from the sea
As a reed-deep pool
Drains back into a ditch.
A buzzard flies
Above the waveless water-line
Not half so high
As fish swim far
Below it.
         Here
The pop-eyed crawlers
Of barely post-glacial ooze
Climb miles up a steep bank
To gain the sea's hard floor.
                  Here
A chartered cruise-ship
Edges up to the quay
As lenses tighten
On wharf and wooden church and waterfall.
A gull or two
Take noisy notice; a dog
Rolls in the gravel track beside the shore;
And the ship slides off again
To New York or Majorca,
Trailing a wake
That rakes no deeper than a chain-harrow
The lake's brittle surface.

But fathoms below
That five-minute ripple,
Below the plankton's arable, the mapped
Approach-route of the salmon,
Far deeper than the shelf
That underpins Norway and the Shetlands,
The locked-in water
Lies still as a rock –
While calculable tides
Roar and storm round the northern latitudes –
Holds its cold
A degree above freezing,
A day's thaw from the last
Dead millennium's calendar of ice.

The fjord's glass veneer
Glows bottle-green all night;
Stars find
Hardly enough dark to shine in;
The clock clicks
Twenty-three day-lit
Bewildering hours.
But drop your watch in that water
And when it touches bottom
It will tell yesterday's time.

Glacier

Its hectares of white
Out of sight from below,
It gropes with one green paw
The rim of the rock-fall.
Each claw
A crunching of bottle-glass,
Opaque and raw,
Splinters as big as a cottage
Cracked between tongs:
A malevolent, rock-crystal
Precipitate of lava,
Corroded with acid,
Inch by inch erupting
From volcanoes of cold.

Slow
Paws creak downwards,
Annexing no
Extra acreage of stone –
For each hooked talon
Is pruned back and pared
By mid-June sun,
And a hundred sluicings
Ooze down the inclined plane
To a wizened, terminal
Half-cone of snow.

The ebb and flow
Of becks that live for a minute
Swishes bath-salt icebergs
Through a shingle moraine –
Where the dandy, grey-rust
Fieldfare rattles
Pebbles in its crop,
And the dwarf cornel
Blinks like a black-eyed buttercup
On the brink of the milk of melting.

Summer now
Out-spills the corrie
With a swill of willow,
But winter's overhang
Retreats not a centimetre –
No fractured knuckle, no
Refrigerated bone
Relinquishes grasp,
Lets slip a finger-hold
To the bland noon's seepage.

For behind black
Rock-terraces and tiers
Slumped winter waits –
For a tilt of earth's axis,
A stretching-out of the polar cold,
To restore the normal, to correct
The climate's misdirection,
Corroborate and order
Mean average temperature
For the last million years.

Midsummer Fires on the Sognefjord

No sunset, no onset of the dark. The eleven-hour-
Long afternoon dims to a hesitant evening.
Overflow pipes from unseen waterfalls
Go on generating electric power;
The glacier greys into cloud; the sea eases almost tideless fingers
    Among the ribs of fells

So named in our Cumbrian tongue, inherited from these
Voes, viks, fosses and mosses. Down by the white
Verandah'd hotel, children enact their fake folk-wedding.
Tourists converse in German and Japanese.
Away on the fjord the oil-can raft burns brighter
    Downwards in the water, while outside wooden

Boat-house and shed, each family lights its fire-sign,
Flapping one to the other like flags along the swing of the shore.
The track through the orchard slowly fills with midnight.
Acres of elder and pale breakers of keck drift white on the dusk's
    brine;
And the map of the puckered coast-line is dirtied over
    To the vague guess of a Vinland chart.

And now, at the day's lowest dip, from aluminium-
Smelting towns, creviced in creeks, and from holiday hutments
      seen
Not even by noon, huge bonfires bore
Tunnels through the mist; a spark lit a millennium
Ago floats up from unchronicled darkness, flies westward
      towards the brown
    Ebb-flowing of the year.

And, maybe, five months from now and the North Sea's width
      away,
I'll watch that spark catch light on a Cumbrian slagbank,
Where boys put matches to heaped sleepers and old bicycle tyres,
And crackers contradict the blacking out of day,
And a smoulder of cardboard and privet exhales, acrid and rank,
    Faint reek of ancestral fires.

Cornthwaite

Cornthwaite, 'the clearing of the corn',
My mother's maiden name – whose umpteenth great-
  grandfather,
Off-come from a northern voe, hacked thorn,
Oak-scrub and birch from rake and beck-bank
To sow his peck of oats, not much of a crop.
Lish as a wind-racked larch, he took his trod
Through landscape nameless still to him, until,
Remembering his own grandfather's talk
Of *tveit* and *dal* and *fiell*,
He scratched those words on the rocks,
Naming the Cymric cwms in a Norse tongue.
The land then named him back.
And here, a millennium later, my baptismal card
Clacks echoes of a clearing beneath cracked
Granite and black pines, where the migrant fieldfare breeds
And the ungregarious, one-flowered cloudberry
Is commoner than crowding bramble. Now,
In my own day's dale, under the slant
Scree of unstable time, I lop,
Chop and bill-hook at thickets and rankness of speech,
Straining to let light in, make space for a word,
To hack out once again my inherited thwaite
And sow my peck of poems, not much of a crop.

Landing on Staffa
or
REGULARITY

Said
Sir Joseph Banks in 1772,
    en route for Iceland,
'Where now is the boast of the architect!
    REGULARITY
the part in which he fancied to exceed
    his mistress, Nature,
is here found in her possession, and here
    has been for ages
undescribed.' – His observations, quoted
    in Pennant's *Tour of*
Scotland and Voyage to the Hebrides,
    brought the describers:
Scott, Keats, Wordsworth, who found the ground crowded
    ('each the other's blight,
hurried and hurrying'); Sir Robert Peel,
    wide brow bared before
'temple not made by hands'; F. Bartholdy-
    Mendelssohn, weaving
wave-shape and cave-shape in quavers – and me
    at a loss for words.
Images proffer themselves – a grooved chip-
    potato cutter,
a wash-tub rubbing board, rolled corduroy,
    the corrugated
iron of a Calvinist Methodist
    chapel, crunched pillars
'bound together like a bunch of matches'

[355]

(Keats said), or ploughed fields
fossilized and up-ended – a dozen
    such knick-knack conceits.
The columns crack into hexagonal
    stools of black basalt;
islands float sweetly, heads scarcely above
    water – the Dutchman[*]
drowned in the Celtic tangle, his hat left
    drifting on the swell.
Mull and Ulva heave like basking seals and
    the tide slides backward.
But the air is blurred with words; pencillings,
    shadings, engravings,
drape huge fish-nets between see-er and seen.
    Quick eyes are dimmed by
a cataract of known appearances.
    The sky pales to a
green familiar aquatint. In the year
    1847,
the Queen and Prince Albert entered the cave
    and haunt it yet. I
turn from the sky-lit gallery, the praised
    portfolio of
A Hundred Famous Views, scurrying south,
    down the ragged rip
of the tartan, to grey unphotographed
    waste acres of West
Cumberland. There, in dark claustrophobic
    winter, I retrace
lonnings once-known to the feet of childhood:
    streets, pavements, schoolyards,
railings, allotments, fields undermined and
    sunken, or horse-tailed

[356]

sumps on the flank of a crumbling pit-bank:
    seeking still to find
one ten-yard panorama, broken fence,
    brown cast-iron tree,
criss-cross curve of slag and slanted grass, or
    just one single stone
that must have lain for ages undescribed –
    and then describe it.

* Dutchman's Hat – a small island off the coast of Mull, visible from Staffa.

[357]

Glen Orchy

Sunday, late summer, 1968:
Mull and Iona behind me and eleven days
Of Highland brightness – Loch Awe electro-plated,
Ben Cruachan chiselled and faceted like cut-glass
In a cubic clarity of air; the River of Orchy,
Subterranean almost, glittering below
Hollowed and pendant shelves of sandy stone.
And everywhere down crag and brae, a tumbling
And cataract of yellowing green, birch and rowan,
Leaf and berry and the churned froth of heather.

                                              Then,
Passing through the village at the foot of the glen,
I stop at a shop with newspapers for sale
And take one, glancing for the cricket scores –
When, like a snapped spring, a familiar name
Headlines clean at me: 'Millom Ironworks
To Close in Four Weeks Time'.

                              And now,
Whenever I remember Glen Orchy,
I see the stretch of light, the waterfalling seasons,
And ten thousand years of after-Ice-Age weathering
Crash on an Arras Wood of smokeless furnace chimneys,
And, blundering among the dead trunks, five hundred men
At one stroke out of work.

On the Dismantling of Millom Ironworks

Child of the clouds! remote from every taint
Of sordid industry thy lot is cast.
William Wordsworth, *The River Duddon,* ii

I laughed once at those words – for there, near where he pondered
On Duddon Bridge, shallow-draft barges shot their ore,
Even in Wordsworth's day, for the charcoal-burning furnace
Sited like a badger's set deep in Duddon woods.
Twenty years on, at the river's mouth, the Hodbarrow miners
Kicked up mountainous mole-hills; a conifer copse of chimneys
Criss-crossed the west with spikes and laterals, and landslides of
    limestone
Walled off all sight of the tide. The river seeped from the marshes
In a flux of haematite. Today, two lifetimes later,
Bled white of every stain of ore, the Duddon rediscovers
Its former channel almost unencumbered – mines
Drowned under stagnant waters, chimneys felled and uprooted,
Slagbanks ploughed down to half their height, all cragginess,
Scrag-end and scree ironed out, and re-soiled and greened over
To long sulky drumlins, dumped there by the look of them
An ice-age ago. They cut up the carcass of the old ironworks
Like a fat beast in a slaughter-house: they shovelled my childhood
On to a rubbish heap. Here my father's father,
Foreman of the back furnace, unsluiced the metal lava
To slop in fiery gutters across the foundry floor
And boil round the workmen's boots; here five generations
Toasted the bread they earned at a thousand degrees Fahrenheit
And the town thrived on its iron diet. On the same ground now
Split foundations moulder in the sea air; blizzards
Of slag-grey dust are blown through broken Main Gate uprights;

Reservoir tanks gape dry beside cracked, empty pig-beds;
And one last core of clinker, like the stump of a dead volcano,
Juts up jagged and unblastable. Stand on the rickety pier,
Look left along the line where gantry and crane and coke-bank
Ten years ago blocked all the view – and now you're staring
Bang at Black Combe. The wind resumes its Right of Way;
Shelduck fly low from feeding-ground to feeding-ground,
No intervening chimneys forcing an upward flight.
In parallel troughs, once dug for the long-since-rotted sleepers
That carried the rails to the tip, cardboard and tags of sacking
Accumulate mulch for dockens and shunting-yards succumb
To a yellow encroachment of ragwort. The town shrinks and
    dwindles.
Old People's Bungalows creak half-way up the hill,
Over a mile away, and privet hedge and hydrangea
Screen out even the memory of smoke and slag. An age
Is pensioned off – its hopes, gains, profits, desperations
Put into mothballs. A hundred years of the Bessemer process –
The proud battery of chimneys, the hell-mouth roar of the
    furnace,
The midnight sunsets ladled across a cloudy sky –
Are archaeological data, and the great-great-great-grandchildren
Of my grandfather's one-time workmates now scrounge this iron
    track
For tors and allies of ore bunkered in the cinders and the
    hogweed.
And maybe the ghost of Wordsworth, seeing further than I can,
Will stare from Duddon Bridge, along miles of sand and mud-
    flats
To a peninsula bare as it used to be, and, beyond, to a river
Flowing, untainted now, to a bleak, depopulated shore.

The Bloody Cranesbill

Every Sunday morning, when I was ten or twelve,
My father and I set off and called on my Uncle Jim
For the weekly fraternal walk. Five minutes' talk with my Auntie,
Then through the allotments, the playing-field, the lonning, out
To the links and warrens and foreshore of the already dying mine
That yet had thirty more years of dying to live through. No longer
The bustle and clang of my father's apprentice days – a thousand
Boots reddening the road at the end of the morning shift:
A Sabbath Day quiet now, no sound but the ricochet,
On the vast, glass, railway-station roof of sky, of the chuff and
    splutter
Of one single locomotive, straining at the week-by-week
Ever-steepening gradient of a hill of unsaleable ore.
The metals undulated bumpily over hillock and hollow
Like a fairground roller-coaster; screes of ore
Dustbinned on to rusty willows; the romanesque brick pit-head
Towers of Number Ten now and then twirled their wheels,
Lifting a couple of miners or half a ton of ore.
We scuffed through a scabbed and scruffy valley of ruddled rocks
To Cumberland's southernmost point, a headland, half-blasted-
    away,
Where the limestone met the tide. Here, on the seaward side,
Wave-action moulds the rocks, thumbs them like plasticine;
Landward the crag splits vertical down to the old workings.
We traversed the yard-wide col between quicksand and quarry,
    and there,
In a cockle-shell dip in the limestone, matted with thrift and rock-
    rose,
Was Sunday's flower, the Bloody Cranesbill, red as the ore

It grew from, fragile as Venetian glass, pencilled with metal-
    thread
Haematite-purple veins. The frail cups lay so gently
On their small glazed saucer-bracts that a whisper would have
    tipped them over
Like emptying tea leaves out. Every Sunday morning
I bent and picked one flower and every time it withered
Before we were half-way home to my Uncle Jim's. Fifty years
    later,
And it's hard to tell there ever was a mine: pit-heads
Demolished, pit-banks levelled, railway-lines ripped up,
Quarries choked and flooded, and all the lovely resistance
Of blackberry, blackthorn, heather and willow grubbed up and
    flattened.
A barren slack of clay is slurried and scaled-out over
All that living fracas of top-soil and rock. A town's
Purpose subsides with the mine; my father and my Uncle Jim
Lie a quarter of a century dead; but out on its stubborn skerry,
In a lagoon of despoliation, that same flower
                                Still grows today.

The Bloody Cranesbill, *Geranium sanguineum*, is fairly common at
a number of places on the Cumbrian coast.

Comprehending It Not

December, 1921. Seven years of age,
And my mother dead – the house in mourning,
The shop shut up for Christmas – I
Was fobbed off to my Grandma's with my Christmas Tree
Bundled under my arm. Out
In the brown packed streets the lamplight drizzled down
On squirming pavements; the after-smell of war
Clung like a fungus to wall and window-sill,
And the backyards reeked of poverty. Boys,
Their big toes squirting through their boots,
Growled out *While Shepherds Watched* to deaf door-knobs,
And the Salvation Army – euphoniums, slung, unplaying –
Stumped the length of the town at the thump of a drum
To cracked Hallelujahs in the Market Square.

I edged past muttering entries, sidled inside the lobby,
And slammed the door on the dark. My Grandma
Banged the floor with her stick to greet me,
Tossed me a humbug and turned again to the goose,
Spluttering on the kitchen range. My four rough uncles
Barged jokily around in flannel shirtsleeves,
Challenged to comic fisticuffs or gripped me
With a wrestler's grip and hyped me and cross-buttocked
In Cumberland-and-Westmorland style – till puffed, at last, and
    weary
Of horse-play and of me, they ripped my Christmas
Tree from its wrapper, unfolded its gaunt
Umbrella frame of branches, stuck candles in the green raffia,
And stood it on the dresser, well out of my reach.

I crouched down by the fire, crunching my humbug,
And scissoring holly and bells from coloured card;
The huff of the smoke brought water to my eyes,
The smell of the goose made me retch. Then suddenly,
The gas plopped out and the house was doused in darkness –
A break in the main and not a chance of repair
Till the day after Boxing Day. Matches rattled;
A twist of paper torn from the *Daily Mail*
Relayed the flame from grate to candle,
And soon, high on the dresser, my Christmas Tree,
Ignited like a gorse-bush, pollened the room with light.

Proud as a proselyte,
I stuffed white wax in the mouth of a medicine bottle,
Pioneered the wild lobby and the attic stairs
And dared the heathen flagstones of the yard,
Bearing my gleam of a gospel. At the scratch of a match,
Christmas crackled up between winter walls,
And Grandma's house was home, her sharp voice called in
    kindness,
And the fists no longer frightened. Tickled at the trick of it,
I 'Merry-Christmased' gas-pipe, gas and gas-men,
'God-blessed' the darkness and pulled crackers with the cold –
Scarcely aware what it was that I rejoiced in:
Whether the black-out or the candles,
Whether the light or the dark.

Hard of Hearing

The landscape of sound
Grows slowly dimmer.
A hush simmers
Up from the ground.
Words are blurred; vowels
Lose almost all their colour;
The lipped and tongued sharp edges
Are smudged and sponged away,
And in an aural darkness
All voices look alike.

Ears staring
Under the twilight,
I grope and blunder
My way to a meaning.
Through the slithering dusk
Walk stumbling, eyes
Strained to the south-
west linger of day.

For behind gloomed tree-trunks
And in shadowy doorways
Unspeaking faces
Gape blankly about me.
Night ties
Bandages round my ears:
Turns verbs
To Blind Man's Buff;
Sends me to black

Coventry in my own skull,
Where not one crack
Of light breaks in
From the town's genial hubbub.

For not from out there
Will come my brightening:
Not from that other dumbness.
Myself is my only
Lamplighter now.
I must illumine my own silence,
Give speech to the blank faces;
If the town won't talk,
Must put words in its mouth.

At the Musical Festival

'He gev it Wigan!' we'd say long ago
When our loved local baritone,
Rendering *The Erl King* or *Ruddier than the Cherry*,
Hurled his voice like an iron quoit
Clean into the Adjudicator's
Union-Jacked box at the back. Never mind
If he was out of tune or muddled his words
Or finished bars ahead of the accompanist –
He'd won his marks, he'd done
What he set out to do; he'd
Given it Wigan.

           The map of England
Was a small one then. London
Was Wembley; Blackpool was holidays;
Manchester was the Test:
All else, a blurred and hachured diagram
Of dialects and geology. We chose
Our bench-marks and points of reference within day-return
Of the one place we knew. It was
Barrow for ships, Whitehaven for coal,
Millom, of course, for men,
And Wigan for a damned good try.

So when, apprehensively, I
Go up for my last class and adjudication – the hall packed,
The audience tense, the examining pencil
Slanted on the unmarked sheet – then,

As I huff and grate and fill my lungs, and eye
The once-for-all starting bell,
God grant me guts to die
Giving it Wigan.

Do You Remember Adlestrop?

Someone, somewhere, must have asked that question – Robert
Frost, may be, or Abercrombie, or, that now
Forgotten genius, John W. Haines, who scarcely
Wrote a line himself but knew the knack
Of making others write them. Someone
Who called at Steep that cold January,' 15,
The poet laid up in bed with a sprained ankle – and 'Yes,
Yes, Yes!' he shouted, as the happy accident
Unsnecked the trapdoor of his memory,
'And willows, willow-herb, and grass'
Burgeoned from a compost of fermenting words –
'Yes, Yes, Yes!' and now everyone remembers.

Is there no question
To fork air into my long-dormant root-stock? No
Fag-card flash of a boy's bright slagbank day,
The wild barley in the back street, the quite impossible catch
That snatched the match and the cup? The questions come,
Blunt and bullying as a bad conscience,
But always the wrong ones. – Do you remember
Stoke Newington, Stockport, Crewe or Solihull?' –
And sadly, guiltily, I reply: 'I'm sorry' –
The trapdoor banged down tight, the compost sour and black
    'No' –
Not even sure if I've ever been there –
'No, I don't remember.'

'Is There Anybody There?' Said the Traveller

I called on my friend in the evening;
    I knocked at the front door.
Three thuds thumped along the lobby –
    No sound more.

No light at the front windows.
    I went round to the back,
Found the rear door open,
    Pushed through to the black

Steep-walled chasm of the kitchen-yard;
    Stumbled on roots
Of Virginia Creeper creeping
    From up-ended chimney-pots.

I groped my way to the window,
    Stood stock-still
While a faint wash of firelight
    Oozed over the window-sill.

I tapped on the glass of the window:
    For answer, not a sound.
But the firelight like a goldfish
    Kept skittering round and round.

It glittered along the shelves of books,
    Titles, to me, unknown,
And down on the black and dizzy wax
    Circling on the gramophone.

And I heard then a hushed conversation,
  Fellow to fellow:
Falsetto chitchat of two flutes,
  The aye-aye of a cello.

And I turned and blundered down the dark,
  Heels scraping backyard loam –
'Mustn't interrupt,' I said:
  'Bach's at home.'

The Safe Side

'It's better to be on the safe side,' my father used to say,
Picking up an umbrella when there was scarcely a cloud in the
   wide
Shop-window of the sky. Now, wearing his greyness, I
Lean on my wordy counter, totting up dots and commas,
Expounding that much and this much if not exactly twice
Yet rather more than once – to be on the safe side.

The Register

Wanting my Birth Certificate and not finding it handy,
I called at the Registry Office for proof that I'd been born,
And the clerk unclasped a volume and pushed it across the table:
'Perhaps you'd like to look at your father's signature?'

Two entries on each page – name, date and parents,
And the Registrar's endorsement: 'Henry Frankland Fox' –
Whose grand-daughter, now my doctor, will maybe one day
Endorse my Death Certificate and clasp up the book with a clang.

Familiar beyond all question, yet not what I'd expected,
A recognized unrecognition faded bluely on the page:
Not a father's and yet a father's, a name that perplexed and
  perturbed me,
Faces and loyalties emerging blurred from a boy's dead world.

It was the hand of James Sharpe, Bachelor of Science,
  Headmaster,
Flourished on each term's report from my twelfth to my
  seventeenth year –
Notifying there, in that last, still almost Edwardian winter,
A daughter's birth a few days before or after mine.

Two st
rict sergeants of my boyhood, guides, guardians, reprimanders,
One loved but not respected, one respected but not loved –
I held their parade-grounds apart, kept one ear for each one's
  instructions,
And their annual Speech Day meeting wrapped embarrassment
  round the Prize.

[373]

As I stand in my father's old shop, among books he could not
   have unpuzzled,
And the hundred yards to the school lead a million miles away,
As the town my mind still lives in crumbles dustily around me –
Joseph Nicholson, James Sharpe, which one am I accountable to?

The New Cemetery

Now that the town's dead
Amount to more than its calculable future,
They are opening a new graveyard

In the three-hedged field where once
Horses of the L.M.S. delivery wagons
Were put to grass. Beside the fence

Of the cricket-ground, we'd watch
On Saturday afternoon, soon after the umpires
Laid the bails to the stumps and the match

Had begun. They'd lead them
Then between railways and St George's precinct – huge
Beasts powerful as the steam

Engines they were auxiliary to:
Hanked muscles oscillating slow and placid as pistons,
Eyes blinkered from all view

Of the half-acre triangle of green,
Inherited for Sunday. But once they'd slipped the harness,
And the pinched field was seen

With its blue lift of freedom,
Those haunches heaved like a sub-continental earthquake
Speeded up in film.

Half a ton of horse-flesh
Rose like a balloon, gambolled like a month-old lamb;
Hind legs lashed

Out at inoffensive air,
Capsized a lorryful of weekdays, stampeded down
Fifty yards of prairie.

We heard the thump
Of hoof on sun-fired clay in the hush between
The bowler's run-up

And the click of the late
Cut. And when, one end-of-season day, they lead me
Up through the churchyard gate

To that same
Now consecrated green – unblinkered and at last delivered
Of a life-time's

Load of parcels – let me fling
My hooves at the boundary wall and bang them down again,
Making the thumped mud ring.

Halley's Comet

My father saw it back in 1910,
The year King Edward died.
Above dark telegraph poles, above the high
Spiked steeple of the Liberal Club, the white
Gas-lit dials of the Market Clock,
Beyond the wide
Sunset-glow cirrus of blast-furnace smoke,
My father saw it fly
Its thirty-seven-million-mile-long kite
Across Black Combe's black sky.

And what of me,
Born four years too late?
Will I have breath to wait
Till the long-circuiting commercial traveller
Turns up at his due?
In 1986, aged seventy-two,
Watery in the eyes and phlegmy in the flue
And a bit bad tempered at so delayed a date,
Will I look out above whatever is left of the town –
The Liberal Club long closed and the clock stopped,
And the chimneys smokeless above damped-down
Furnace fires? And then will I
At last have chance to see it
With my own as well as my father's eyes,
And share his long-ago Edwardian surprise
At that high, silent jet, laying its bright trail
Across Black Combe's black sky?

THE CANDY-FLOSS TREE

(1984)

Off to Outer Space Tomorrow Morning

You can start the Count Down, you can take a last look;
You can pass me my helmet from its plastic hook;
You can cross out my name in the telephone book –
    For I'm off to Outer Space tomorrow morning.

There won't be any calendar, there won't be any clock;
Daylight will be on the switch and winter under lock.
I'll doze when I'm sleepy and wake without a knock –
    For I'm off to Outer Space tomorrow morning.

I'll be writing no letters; I'll be posting no mail.
For with nobody to visit me and not a friend in hail,
In solit'ry confinement as complete as any gaol
    I'll be off to Outer Space tomorrow morning.

When my capsule door is sealed and my space-flight has begun,
With the teacups circling round me like the planets round the sun,
I'll be centre of my gravity, a universe of one,
    Setting off to Outer Space tomorrow morning.

You can watch on television and follow from afar,
Tracking through your telescope my upward shooting star,
But you needn't think I'll give a damn for you or what you are
    When I'm off to Outer Space tomorrow morning.

And when the rockets thrust me on my trans-galactic hop,
With twenty hundred light-years before the first stop,
Then you and every soul on earth can go and blow your top –
    For I'm off to Outer Space tomorrow morning.

[381]

Road Up

What's wrong with the road?
Why all this hush? –
They've given an anaesthetic
In the lunch-hour rush.

They've shaved off the tarmac
With a pneumatic drill,
And bandaged the traffic
To a dead standstill.

Surgeons in shirt-sleeves
Bend over the patient,
Intent on a major
Operation.

Don't dare sneeze!
Don't dare shout!
The road is having
Its appendix out.

I Don't Believe in Ghosts

I don't believe in ghosts.
            No matter how they talk
Of an old man with whiskers
            White as chalk,

Who sits beside a window
            Above the dark yards,
Dealing a round
            Of invisible cards.

Go in if you want to!
            Creep up the stairs,
Build a makeshift table
            Of two broken chairs;

Switch on your pocket torch;
            Play three-handed rummy,
With one empty place
            And no one for dummy;

Hold back your aces;
            Don't try to win.
See if the old joker
            Will want to join in.

You'll deal yourself a blank hand!
            Never you fear!
I don't believe in ghosts –
            But I'm staying here.

Ten Yards High

I'm ten yards high.
The jackdaws fly
Out from the chimney-pots
As I stride by.
'Clumsy clown!'
The mothers cry
When I push down the washing
With the jut of my thigh.
'Look where you put
Your foot!' – but I
Don't give a hoot
If the line is in a tangle
Or the sheets are apple-pie.
Let them hang their clothes to dry
Out of reach of my boot.
For they're quite beneath my notice
From this window-sill, skylight,
Roof-line height.
When the weather's chill
Smoke from fires
Brings tears to my eye,
And if I stand still
The sparrows fight
To shelter in the eaves
Of my collar and tie.
I peep in dormer-casements,
See beds unmade
And tights flung awry –
The girls draw the curtains

As I creep by!
I bend down and pry
Into upper flights
Of double-deck buses,
Get an eyeful of the trouble
The conductor misses;
Stare straight in the face
Of the Town Hall Clock;
Strike a match on the roof
Of the Market block;
Bump into the church,
Hold tight to the spire,
Look down on the churchyard
Where one day I'll lie
In a grave as long
As a cokernut shy.
And when I die
Will the sextons all
Knock off and down spades
At the sight of my
Unburied length?
Will they call it a day
And demand extra pay?
And will everyone say:
'He was a man
Of such power and strength
He could toss that tower
Right up to the sky.
Oh, he'll be a hero
A thousand years!
And the reason why? –
He was ten yards high.'

Five-inch Tall

I'm five-inch tall.
I dive and crawl
Into the jungle
Of the uncut lawn.
Fawn-coloured stems
Of plate-size daisies
Sway round my head
In a tangle of weed.
A monstrous, pop-eyed,
Dinosaur snail
Stares out from the dome
Of his mobile home,
Leaving a slime-trail
Wide as a drain.
In distant, dark-furred
Thickets of twitch,
A cricket whirs
Like a motor-mower.

I creep from the lower
Foothills of lawn
Into a conifer
Forest of horse-tails,
Where writhing, boa-
constrictor worms
Coil round fern-trunks
Or heave through the soil.
Undaunted, unshaken,
I break from the shade

To a lake of sunlight –
Five-inch tall
And the heir of acres,
With all the walled dukedom
To call my own.

But high on a pear-tree
A pocket falcon,
With bragging, flaunted,
Red-flag breast,
Is poised to strike;
Dives down and pounces –
Grappling-iron talons
And beak like a pike.
Shaken, daunted,
Arms over my chest,
I cringe and turn tail;
Off like a shot
To the vegetable plot,
Helter-skelter for the shelter
Of broccoli and kale;
Yielding the field
To red-rag robin –
For safety is all
When you're five-inch tall.

In a Word

Sun –

          In a word –

                   beams

Rain –

          A green bird –

                   drops

Snow –

          White and furred –

                   flakes

Thunder –

          All heard –

                   claps

Applause, applause, applause,

          Because

Something's always happening

          In a word.

Turn on the Tap

Turn on the tap!
See a waterfall
Spout from the pipe:
A thin rill
That spills down a gill
Where salmon shoot
The rapids upward,
Fins clinging
To rock-crack and root.
See cool drops drool
From an upland pool,
Where rice-grain bubbles
Ooze through the mud,
And the silt stirs
In the troubled current
Clogging the stems
Of bog-bean and rush.
Neither willow nor alder
Breaks the bare shore;
But the still lake-water
Reflects the black
Jag-edge of crag,
The tumbled cap
Of the summit cairn –
Turn on the tap:
You're drinking a tarn.

Turn on the tap!
Hear the west wind

Howl up from Ireland,
Skimming the scum
Off the simmering seas.
Keep your ears skinned
For the whistling kettle
Of the hot Atlantic,
For the rattle of hail
Like a clout of dried peas
Flung on a drum.
The oceans steam
In the sun's sweaty breath;
Mist-wreaths settle
On every humped hill;
As huge sponges of clouds
Wring themselves out
Into pot-hole and spout.
England's long backbone
Is drenched to the marrow,
As the funnels of storm
Pour down on the fells
And swill into narrow
Channels and runnels
Of ditch and drain –
Turn on the tap:
You're drinking rain!

Put on More Coal

Put on more coal!
See ferrets of fire
Glide through the age-old
Forest glades;
See horse-tails higher
Than a chimney stack
Spire up and crash
Down cindery screes;
See an up-the-flue draught
Breeze round the boles
Of fossilized ferns,
Turning the ash
Bonfire-bright.
Put on more coal:
You're burning trees!

Put on more coal!
See caves of rubble
Bubble and crack
Under weight of flame;
See long-dead miners,
Bare-backed and black,
Turn in their graves,
Awake to work again,
And ram at the rock
In the pit of the night.
Stir up the fire!

Each hundredweight won
From a fight with the dark.
Put on more coal:
You're burning men!

The Man from the Advertising Department

There's more to see
In the next field.
Not much here
But grass and daisies
And a gulley that lazes
Its way to the weir –
Oh there's much more to see
In the next field.

There are better folk
In the next street.
Nobody here
But much-of-a-muchness people:
The butcher, the blacksmith,
The auctioneer,
The man who mends the weathercock
When the lightning strikes the steeple –
But they're altogether a better class
In the next street.

There'll be more to do
In the next world.
Nothing here
But breathing fresh air,
Loving, shoving, moving around a bit,
Counting birthdays, forgetting them, giving
Your own little push to the spin of the earth;
It all amounts to
No more than living –

But by all accounts
There'll be more to do
And more to see
And VIP neighbours
In the next world.

PREVIOUSLY UNPUBLISHED
AND
UNCOLLECTED POEMS

From On the Shore

The bathers are gone; a man is gathering driftwood.
  And the sea ebbs through a brown autumn,
Through mists curled and fragile as periwinkle's shell,
  Through skies blotched like a mackerel,
Till winter aluminiums the waves with a glint of seaholly
  And its thistle-bud hint of blue.
But among sand-blocked wharves and stagnant docks
  The metal waters rust,
And crank up and down like an old chain swinging in the wind
  From a derelict lobster-armed crane.
And stepping over worm-eaten sleepers, past the walls
  Of the silent foundry, come the
    men with hands in pockets
    humpbacked to the world,
    locked out of mine and mill
    by a machine by an explosion by a jump
    in prices by a change in fashion
    by a director's whim by a slump
    in a glutted world by a poverty-
    strangled demand by investor's
    mumps by a war by a peace
    by profits by corners by swindlers
    by deals scoops ramps thefts lies,
    barred from the fields and the hills
    for the grazing sheep for the grouse
    while varicose wicks knot
    the grass for lack labour;
    craftsman robbed of his tools
    labourer of his plough all

of the savage right of toil
to till the soil and pluck
the fruit and kill for food;
now father dependent on son
brother on brother man
on men unknown, hands
reft of pickaxe and spade
grudgingly take the dole
of another's hewing and digging.
The light has ebbed, life has waned, the sea
shrinks back into its shell.
I walk far out on the marshes till the dykes behind me
scurry from the eye like a scared rat.

February—March 1938

Song: the Wind and the Window

Tell me, Wind, and Window, tell me,
   Is it smoke or dusk or dust
Gusted along yellow pavements
    Out of hollow chimneys thrust?
      Powder of the chalky street
       Ground by hobnail and bare foot?
       Tell me, you that sight
       You that breathing gave?

Tell me, Wind, as you blow westwards
   Towards my left hand and the sea
Is it chapel bell from fellside,
    Cycle bell or stroke of 3?
      Is it groaning in the street
       Organed by an unknown throat?
       Lungs of day and night
       Tell, if you can tell?

Tell me, Window, all the wonder
   Of the bobbined winding hours,
People cut from cardboard, spellbound,
    Prams and pigeons and torn flowers,
      Puppet pageant of the street,
       Is it truth or is it sleight?
       Eyes that sift the light
       Tell, if you can tell.

When my breath is broken, Wind, oh
   When my sight is shuttered too,

Will you blow, Wind? Window, will you
Open still for others' view?
Oh are noises in the street
Only echoes of my note?
Flickerings of fate –
Breath upon the sill.

5 July 1938

Prayer for a Political Meeting

Unto your mercy, Sir, we remember
   the people of China and Spain:
Who engage in our struggle, who make their bodies
   the margin in our books where theory
     is checked and proved or rejected.
Greater love has no man than this
   that out of his trustfulness and humility
   and out of his helplessness and simplicity
   and out of his blindness and stupidity
     he shall give his life for what he does not know.

Sir, if the struggle is inevitable
   we do not ask that you should avert the struggle;
Sir, if the struggle comes
   we do not ask that we should be exempted from it,
For we are not the sort to sit at home and hope for the best,
   to shelter in the neutral hills, in the schoolroom or the
       monastery;
We are the sort that must have our finger in the pie,
   that must follow some leader wherever he may lead;
We are the sort that must be up and doing
   even to our undoing.
We do not speak of this as being worthy of praise,
   but we know it is our nature.

Sir, we do not ask for victory;
   we ask that in victory you will not desert us;
That the cities we shall build, our powerhouses, our factories,
   our dynamos which hold in leash the lightning,

Our navigation towers which look into the level thunder,
   our blocks of flats for thousands upon thousands of workers,
Shall not lack the Grace that once gave permanence
   to a ramshackle stable at Bethlehem.
Sir, we do not ask for victory:
   we ask that in victory you will not desert us,
      nor in defeat abandon us.

For victory without you is no longer victory
   nor are we defeated if you are with us in defeat.

New English Weekly, 12 January 1939

No Man's Land

I have heard crack the warning
Ice, alone,
By the debated track
Scotched on bare stone.

I have traversed the salient,
Been aware of
The cairn beyond the next cairn,
The menace in a sheep's cough;

The snaring bog,
The threat of nightfall,
The sniper's cue
In the snipe's call;

The whisper like a silence
In the hollow of the force
That booms over the cleft ledge
Bombarding its course.

The alert crag,
The skulking mist:
Is it behind that or this,
The clenched unflinching fist?

What is it?
What is there?
At bay on startled heels,
I challenge the blank air.

Stockstill. Take my bearings: I know
Every quarry in the valley, every chock-
stone in the gully, every gutter in the ghyll . . .
I do not know that rock.

Faltered;
Turned back.
Sought cover beside a friendly dyke,
Or a furry haystack.

Nor does the camouflage of summer
Allay my doubt:
From among the zigzag bracken
The snake's head looks out.

In the blue night sky
Above the bilberry knoll
The unthawed stars
Point to the wintry Pole.

I have fled to the lowlands,
Called my thoughts in;
Entrenched between houses
I have saved my skin;

With a thousand watts
Patrolled the dark;
Caged my linnet,
Policed the park.

But on the skyline
The gaunt fell
Taunts me with slate shoulders.
And I know well

I shall break this truce
And one day again
I shall go to the black tarn
Slaked with rain;

The unknown I shall know,
Though how to do
May take all my living to learn,
Or dying too.

Southern Review, Autumn 1940

Now That I Have Made my Decision

NOW THAT I HAVE MADE MY DECISION and felt God on my tongue
It is time that I trained my tongue to speak of God;
Not with pretended wisdom, nor with presumption,
But as a tree might speak of rain, that no resumption
Of yesterday's words may sour the sweet grapes of His blood.

Now that I have burned my boats on an ebbing sea
That once was quicksand but returned to would-be sand of hell,
It is time that I cease to stare towards the horizon for a goal,
But gear my gaze to the near path cogged out for my soul,
Or step if it need through the black bracken of the untracked fell.

16 October 1940

Sonnet for Good Friday

The time's a tree to hang from as I die,
While steel thorns spike my wrists into the wood,
And from my running wounds the anemone
Drips on the passive soil in scabs of blood.
There were not lacking those to thrust out tongue,
Nor those to squabble for my scanty gear,
Nor those to wish me strength to suffer long
And break my bones when I could bear no more.
Malevolence of man's secreted sins
Is nothing to the agony of sap
That rises to redemption in my veins
And gimlets all my flesh with buds of hope.
    Death is less terrible than third-day birth,
    When blood shall blossom on the holy earth.

An Anthology of Religious Verse
ed. Norman Nicholson, Penguin Books, 1942

Poem

I would make a poem
Precise as a pair of scissors, keen,
Cold and asymmetrical, the blades
Meeting like steel lovers to define
The clean shape of the image.

I would make a poem
Organic as an orchid, red
Flowers condensed from dew, with every lobe
Fitted like a female to receive
The bee's fathering head.

I would make a poem
Solid as a stone, a thing
You can take up, turn, examine and put down;
Bred of the accident of rain and river,
Yet in its build as certain as a circle,
An axiom of itself.

Outposts, Summer 1949

On Suspected Dry Rot in the Roof
of a Parish Church

It might have been a sandstorm built it – lish
Lifting and spiralling of wind that drew
The rusty iron filings of the desert
   High in magnetic air;
It might have been the red sirocco blew
   Those arches there.

This whirlwind stratified mid in its whirl,
This mirage you can break your ankles on,
This dried-blood delta of permian denudation,
   Proud paleozoic
Corpse of a desert mummified into stone,
   Hierarchic and heroic,

This act, this accident, this church – has felt
No change of climate, known no count of clock.
The quarry sleeps with its great mouth open, drooling
   Daisies, senile with slime,
Emptied of centuries as well as rock,
   Emptied of time.

But upward, look at the roof! When the heavy sun
Pulls the tide of light west of the swell, free
Of the prayer-sodden, green-mould angels on the blind aisle,
   See the gray in the grain.
Someone's left the cold tap dripping in the belfry –
   Look at the stain!

Fungus probes deeper than the wind that blows
Over these vertical dunes. Life, rotting on the bare
Detritus of a dead star, blossoms as the microbe,
    Corrupting beam and band;
Spirit and spore under bright infected air
    Plant gardens in sand.

The New Statesman, 25 July 1953

The Affirming Blasphemy

at Mexborough, South Yorkshire
'America's all right, but I like Mexborough best', A.F. aged 10,
on her return from Connecticut.

Good God, girl, yes! For what's a continent
Compared to this? – A lank, trans-puberty canal
You can half hop over or plumb with a stone on a string:
Brown as a tabby-cat, persistent as a tom,
At the lock-gates waiting for the sluice to open,
Then with a bristle and whisk of fur,
Tail over tip and away. Or what's the Atlantic
Compared to this? – Bull, blue-blowing whales,
With dorsal fins of coal, leaning and careening
Their barnacled flanks against the banks. The wake
Seeps back from ash-path and allotment, leaving,
Stranded, a corymb of starfish on the ragwort stems.
Look! by the lock-bridge now (Van Gogh in sepia)
Gannets are tethered to the keeper's stocking line,
Feathering the blue-rinse wind. Eastward, volcano stacks
Are brushing picture poems on a Japanese
Rice-paper sky, whence now the sun –
Back home again – peers like a one-eyed collier
Grinning through his grime.

                    Good God, girl, yes!
And that's the why of it, the chart and the charity: –
God and his goodness.

                    'Good God, man, no!'
The miner chews his words and gobs in the water,

[411]

Sealing a put-and-take negation
With the world's one Yes. A casual blasphemy
Tricks the tongue into truth, and the unwilled meaning
Shines ambiguous as a smile through anger: –
Good and its god-ness.

                              The world's one No
Drags cold across the land; a harrow of iron
Rips up the soil and grapples deep in the rock.
Trees are charred in the freezing wind; a black
Hoar of soot settles on leaf and petal,
Congealing all to mineral nullity. Coal-
black ice, in packs and fractures, retched
Up pit-shafts' frozen geysers, binds
The lie against the light. Glaciers of denial
Grind outwards from the black, blaspheming Pole:
'Good God, man, no! No good,
No God.'

                        The truth, against the dark,
Flares suddenly. Glaciers crack and the black ice
Melts. From under the tundra of despondency
A carboniferous humus flames into fruit.
Hundred-million-year-long latent spores
Germinate green in a burning spring; ferns
Unfurl in hearth and furnace – crackling bracken
And spleenworts of fire. On winter slagscapes
Smoky-branched larches drop their clinker cones,
Lockets and nuggets of sun. The world's one flower
Blooms on the broken fronds of a flowerless age.
Shale calyx raising a combustible corolla
To the sky's one seed.

Then let the seed's one star
Flower brightest in your own eyes. Polish the cobbles;
Make scrap-iron shine with a burnish and foil of joy.
Blow pipefuls of rainbows at the spouting barges;
Play tig with the wind; hopscotch and hunt the tow-path;
With cruetty legs kick salt-mustard-pepper
Through skipping-rope twirls of smoke.
For now the lie burns back against itself;
The blasphemy affirms. To surprised skies
The one sun rises out of the night-black pit,
And the mocked, mug-made, mutilated earth cries:
Good (Yes, girl) God!

Times Literary Supplement, 10 December 1954

Peculiar Honours

The wind will be there,
  In the wondering house,
  Mousing and mumbling
At the Child's hair,
Scaring jackdaws of smoke
  To the chimneypot sky –
The wind will be there.
  But where, Lord, am I?

Clay will be there
  In the hip-and-haw brick,
  Cold earth autumned
By the fire's glare;
And mud bright as onyx
  Will slate the roof dry –
They will be there.
  But where, where am I?

Trees will be there
  In the boughs of the rafters,
  And wild sticks wickered
For the Child's chair;
With graining and knot
  In panel and ply –
Every tree of the air
  And the birds of its joy.

Man's self will be there,
　　His flesh and his nature,
　　His creature condition,
His brag and his prayer;
Encompassed and climaxed
　　In limbs of a boy
Mankind is all there
　　And there, now, am I.

Church Times, 24 December 1954

Of This Parish

Here on the churchyard hill the dead lie higher
    (Under the winter
    Heliotrope, the garish
    Wreaths, the slanter
    Two o'clock shadow of the spire)
Than all the tall electors of this parish.

Not in the ore that fed them or the slate that sheltered,
    But in brown smoulder
    Of glacial clay
    The dead burn colder;
    While rain and tears are skeltered
Down through the drains of the town to the sump of the bay.

We dump the wreaths in a ventilated bin:
    Soused in paraffin –
    Tulips, chrysanthemums,
    Premature blossoming thorn,
    Find in the flames
A short cut to the Resurrection Morn.

The Grapevine, 1956

Under the Auspices of the County Council

It was the hum
Of silence drew me to the crumbling
Quarry in the yellow drench of autumn –
Birk of silver-gilt and sycamores
With flecked paint peeling off. November
Turns its blowlamp on the timber
Till the quarry walls are drifted, flag to beam,
With blisters and burnings of leaf. Oranges and lemons
Ring downward in a chime of colour from
The steeples of the rocks. Yet it is shadow I remember,
Unlit by fern: the hollow where an old steam
Roller (its silent fly-wheels humming
In a paralysis of power) waits for the green moment
To break out from the tent of rust and bramble
And bring an unearned meaning to this poem.
Time and Tide, 16 March 1957

Daily Work

Come, workers for the Lord
And lift up heart and hand;
Praise God, all skill at bench and board,
Praise, all that brain has planned.

When Christ to manhood came
A craftsman was he made
And served his glad apprentice time
Bound to the joiner's trade.

When Christ on Calvary
Drank down his cruel draught,
The men who nailed him to the tree
Were men of his own craft.

So, God, our labour take,
From spite and greed set free;
May nothing that we do or make
Bring ill to man or thee.

All workers for the Lord,
Come sing with voice and heart;
In strength of hands be God adored
And praised in power of art.

100 *Hymns For Today*, 1969

[418]

They Said

When he was five
His puppy died.
They said:
Poor Little fellow.

When he was ten
His mother died.
They said:
It's hard on the lad.

When he was thirty
His father died.
They said:
It comes to all of us.

When he was fifty
His brother died.
They said:
He'll soon get over it.

When he was seventy
His wife died.
They said:
He hasn't much to live for.

When he was eighty
He died.
They said:
It's a happy release.

1969

Better Wait

Better wait
Till you start school.
You're too small yet.
The other boys are all bigger than you.
They're too rough for you.
You'll only hurt yourself.
Better wait
Till you start school.

Better wait
Till you go to the Seniors.
You're still too young to be safe on a bike.
There's so much traffic.
The roads are a death-trap.
And make sure first of your eleven-plus.
Better wait
Till you go to the Seniors.

Better wait
Till you leave school.
You need your sleep.
And you've got your homework.
And what do you want with girls at your age.
There'll be plenty of chance for all that later.
Better wait
Till you leave school.

Better wait
Till you're married.

Don't rush it.
You've all your life before you.
And once you've made your mind up
You'll have to lie on it.
Better wait
Till you're married.

Better wait
Till the kids grow up.
There's more than you to think of now.
You've got responsibilities.
You've got ties.
Somebody has to do the donkey-work.
Somebody has to sacrifice something.
Better wait
Till the kids grow up.

Better wait
Till you've retired.
You can't afford to ease off the pressure.
Keep your eye on that pension.
Keep your hand off those brochures.
There's always next year for this year's holiday.
Better wait
Till you've retired.

Better wait
A bit longer.
Try to keep active.

Try to keep cheerful.
Don't give in to the old Anno Domini.
It's not time yet to start putting your feet up.
Better wait
Till you're dead.

1969

Tromsø

Tromsø, warehouse and waiting-room of the Arctic:
Streets of gravel and dust-topped permafrost,
With magpies skittering, perky as bantams –
    It's dark there now.

The longest concrete bridge in Europe
Cat-backs the stockfish fjord from wharfside to wharfside;
The mountain railway that wasn't working when *we* called
    won't be working now.

Glacier-fed waterfalls in dynamo'd daleheads
Sprinkle the darkness with powder-ice glitter;
Raw noons are eked out to the moon's arrival;
    Daylight's on ration now.

But, midwinter here, as the tea-time sun is beaming
Its million candle-power along the haar of chimneys,
Not the light's dazzle but one black image blinds me:
    It's pitch-dark in Tromsø now.

Phoenix, Summer 1970

Pearlwort

Like a tuft of tangled wool
Or the tatter of an astrakhan collar,
Parachuted down on the bowling green
Or drifted against the bricks of an old wall,
Inconspicuous as a money-spider:
Sagina procumbens,
The herb of the pearl.

The oyster forms a pearl to protect itself –
A shelly secretion of calcium carbonate
Round an itching-point of grit.
This is the grit without the pearl!

It anchors its suckers in the skin of the earth,
Limpeting to one square inch of soil or gravel.
Water it with weed-killer,
Prod it with garden prongs;
Light a bonfire over it,
Dump cinders, old bicycles and cardboard boxes,
And when the rain swills the dead grass clear again,
Pearlwort will still be there:
The little, hairy, irritating wart
That won't be scratched away.

You can't say it blooms –
All it has for flowers are green funnels,
No bigger than the pupil of your eye,
To let sunlight into the stalks.
You can't say it fruits –

The stems send down their suckers at every joint,
Dragging themselves along the grain of the ground,
Holding on without need of pollen or seed.

You can hardly say it grows –
Looking dry and yellow in spring
And fresh as a week-old sprig when it's almost dead.
It just persists.

A bit like a poet.

A Garland for Leonard Clark on his 75th Birthday,
Enitharmon, 1980

Old Railway Sidings, Millom

Here once, three times a day and three days out from Durham,
Sixty ten-ton-wagon conveyances of coke were shunted
Down to the Bessemer furnace, and, marshalled the other way,
Wagons from the mines stocked high with red pickle cabbage of
　　ore,
Routed for Sheffield or Wales. The black and the red met,
　　checked,
Side-stepped one another like chessmen as the day-shift swiped
　　the board.
A squat slate terrace on its sunken pavement (bedroom windows
Level with the passing axles) peeked out into smoke and coke-
　　dust-
Where now huge double-glazings stare uninterrupted to the fells,
And the lilacs of doorway and lintel take four times as long to
　　blacken.
April is cindery here, and the privet, ashen and gray
Long before it's green. And yet the spring burns through
Like damped-down fire in a pit-bank. Tussocks and tufts and
　　ravels,
Too young to say their names, un-knot from the black soil;
Codlins-and-cream and comfrey crane up from hairy necks
Through collars of bicycle wheels and broken pots. The earth
Scratches itself awake. And I, picking my way
Through a tanglement of blackberry and rusty iron scrap,
See, at my feet, a scattering of white, as of blackthorn blossom
Fallen or the droppings of a bird smaller even than a wren –
And, stooping close, bring quickly into focus a cress of the dunes,
The vernal whitlow-grass, pegging its pigmy claim
A long way out from home. And suddenly a wind lifts up,

Westerly from the Irish Sea, and the tang of the ebb-tide's iodine
Startles the nose and stings the eyes; the clanging cries
Of shelduck and greater blackback fracture the town's dull
    drone.
A thousand years before they built the sidings, the high
Tides stretched up to here on the full and the new moon,
    swamping
The salt-mud lonning we squared the terrace on. And now,
As the temporary tenancy of miners and smelters runs out, the sea
Turns ground landlord again, asserts its ancient rights,
Scrubs out the grubby reminders of seven generations of off-
    comes,
Announcing its intentions with a flower no bigger than a
    whitebait's eye.

A Garland for The Laureate: Poems Presented to
Sir John Betjeman on His 75th Birthday
Celandine Press, 1981

Epithalamium for a Niece

'Who gives this woman to this man?'
The parson asks, and one man can,
According to the liturgy,
Rightly reply. And many more,
If saying 'I do' were the door
To show their daughters out, would say
It now and twenty times a day.
But with 'I do' or merely 'Me',
Failing the Prayer Book's nudge, who'd claim
Just cause or just justification
To dare the pride of giving? Let
Church and choir and congregation
Silent remain and the reply
Come from some other than the 'I'
That hesitates at 'Do'. The wind
Might say: 'I gave her breath'; the sky:
'I gave the light to see her by';
Soil and humus, stem and stone:
'We gave the calcium for the bone,
Carbohydrates, minerals, those
Hormones and genes and chromosomes
That chose her sex and shaped her nose'.
Water might lap and lip: 'From me
Venus was born, so why not she?'
But neither earth nor sky nor water
Speak sponsorship for this their daughter.
So in the eternity before
'I do' is done, and while the air
Waits on the Prayer Book's questionnaire,

Let silence ring its loud reply:
'She gives herself – what can a man ask more?'

London Magazine, July 1984

Comet Come

For Peggy

It's here at last. Eyes in the know
Had spotted it two years ago,
A microscopic smut on film.
The probes are launched; binoculars
Lurk ready on dark attic stairs,
Waiting and hoping. But for what?
For Giotto's Star of Bethlehem,
Or that bright threatener in the sky
That twanged a spike through Harold's eye
And dumped a Norman on the throne?
Those nightly-watched incendiary flashes
That put a match to London town
And burnt the stews and steeples down,
Breeding the Plague among their ashes,
Or in black, after-chapel air,
The admonitory naphtha-flare
Our fathers saw, whose motto read:
'War coming and King Edward dead.'

Prompt as an actor to his cue,
It teeters feebly into view,
A dirty snowball, chimney-high,
Faint phosphorescence in the sky,
Not up to candle-power – a barely
Distinguishable blur, as if
God in an artist's dab and doubt
Had sketched a star and thumbed it out.
We search and strain – but with a hiss

The clouds swish over like a curtain,
Blacking the scene out, and, uncertain
Which smudge is which, we rub sore eyes,
Wondering why on earth we've waited
Seventy years and more for this.
Where is the pride of mathematics
When magi and magicians (no
Newton or Einstein in their credo)
Can manage to see more than we do?

Anxious astronomers protest:
Give them a month, they'll know just what
The frozen core is made of, test
The fluorescence tailing from it,
Fanned out in the solar wind,
Promising faithfully the comet
Will shine as it has never shone
In Twenty Hundred and Sixty One.
(By which time they'll contrive together
Even to guarantee the weather.)

But in that year of Sixty-One
What will the comet look down on?
A wiser world, or one unpeopled,
Dead as the asteroidal dust
It hoovers, on its orbit, through?
Will telescopes still sweep the view
With no one to stare up them? Must
Satellites circle aimlessly
A circling satellite? Or when
Halley returns next time but ten
Will toe-and finger-counting men,
On unpolluted islands, pray,
In awe and wonder once again:
'Thy comet come, O Lord, Amen.'

The Listener, 13 March 1986

There's a War On

'Don't you know
There's a war on?'
They used to say
Forty years ago,
Whenever we threw away
Waste paper we should have saved, or dropped
Two lumps of sugar in our tea,
Or, from an undrawn blind,
Let a windowful of light
Beam out into the night –
'There's a war on!
Has nobody told you?'

No war now.
Clouds
Float calmly over
Barricades in the street, feet
Crashing on broken glass, crowds
Setting fire to cars,
Bombs in the Market Square;
Girls, old men, soldiers, faces hot
With anger, presidents shot;
A child sobbing in the cold night air –
There's a peace on!
Has nobody told them?

New Angles: Book One, O.U.P., 1987

How's That?

How's that?
Asks the bowler –
Pad before wicket,
Feet splayed awry, wrist higher
Than shoulder, a comic cartoon of cricket –
Not out,
Says the Umpire.

How's that?
Ask the Neighbours –
Sacked from his job with the Dole Queue for a hobby,
Cheques bounced by the Bank, wife
Run off with the lodger, bailiff's in the lobby –
Not out.
Says Life.

How's that?
Asks the Justice –
Nabbed red-handed, stranded with no hope,
And a hundred willing hands ready to shove
A branded man still lower down the slope –
Not out.
Says Love.

How's that?
Asks the Doctor –
Four score years and ten,

With a gurgle in the bronchials, a growling in the breath,
Appealing for a re-play, life over once again –
Out,
Says Death.

New Angles: Book One, O.U.P., 1987

The Contract

They offered me a contract when my turn came to be born,
A water-tight agreement, all well and truly drawn:
The guarantee on parchment with a flourish six-inch long
And a great fat gob of sealing-wax as big as any gong –
    But I didn't read the small print at the bottom.

A free land to live in and God's free air to breathe;
Free milk, free specs, free dentures before I'd lost my teeth;
A free education in grammar school or college,
And a free encyclopaedia to the whole of modern knowledge –
    But I didn't read the small print at the bottom.

A Five-Star Mental Clinic with free soap for blowing bubbles
And psychologists in every room to listen to my troubles;
A gold ring for my finger, for my mouth, a silver spoon,
And a ticket for a non-return excursion to the moon –
    But I didn't read the small print at the bottom.

I was analysed and treated with a mild electric shock.
They brought me here by rocket and took back a lump of rock;
Gave me a litre of oxygen and left me on my own
Playing marbles with the polished glassy pebbles of the moon –
    'Cause I hadn't read the small print at the bottom.

Oh, they carried out their promises, said what they had to say.
For however free your life is, you've always got to pay.
You sign along the dotted line and your name's stamped out in
    black!

You're born into a one-way street and there's no turning back –
So always read the small print at the bottom.

New Angles: Book Two, O.U.P., 1987

Textual Variations

'Egremont'

l. 17 'Picts' reads 'Scots' in *Selected Poems* (1966).

'Cleator Moor'

l. 25 'waggon' reads 'wagon' in *Selected Poems* (1966).

'To The River Duddon'

l. 4 'Hardknott' reads 'Hard Knott' in *Selected Poems* (1966).

l. 9 'a pension on the civil list' reads 'a government sinecure' in
   Selected Poems (1966).

l. 45 'lass' is omitted in *Selected Poems* (1966).

l. 48 'Like scree sheer into the sand, and seen the tide' reads 'Like
   scree into the sand, and watched the tide' in *Selected Poems*
   (1966).

l. 67 'frothy' is omitted in *Selected Poems* (1966).

ll. 68–9 are omitted in *Selected Poems* (1966).

'The Blackberry'

ll. 19–20 are omitted in *Selected Poems* (1966).

'For St James, 1943'

l. 9 'holy' is omitted in *Selected Poems* (1966).

'The Raven'

l. 11 'lyle' reads 'lile' in *Selected Poems* (1966).

'Thomas Gray in Patterdale'
l. 3 'ghylls' reads 'gills' in *Selected Poems* (1966).
'Across The Estuary'
Section 11 is omitted from *Selected Poems* (1966).
Section III *l.* 31 'Like sand beneath my feet' reads 'Beneath my feet' in
Selected Poems (1966).

THE POT GERANIUM

'Scarf Gap, Buttermere'
On the Contents page of the 1954 edition the poem is entitled only
'Scarf Gap', but the poem itself is entitled 'Scarf Gap, Buttermere'. In
Selected Poems (1966) the title was changed to 'Scarth Gap,
Buttermere' which is the name on Ordnance Survey maps and in
Nicholson's *Greater Lakeland*.
l. 24 'Melbreak' reads 'Mellbreak' in *Selected Poems* (1966).
'The Undiscovered Plant'
l. 11 'pupil; only' reads 'pupil. Only' in *Selected Poems* (1966).
'The Seven Rocks'
Selected Poems (1966) omits all the introductory notes and all the
Latin names in the sub-titles. It also omits the note on Inglewood.

A LOCAL HABITATION

'The Whisperer'
ll. 23–5 are omitted from *Selected Poems* (1982).
'On The Closing of Millom Ironworks'
*l.*15 is omitted from *Selected Poems* (1982).

Index of titles